"A beautifully written memoir about two cats who suddenly show up, move in, and set up housekeeping. As human and feline lives slowly intertwine, it's ultimately unclear who is nurturing whom as they slowly become a family. The story of Kit Kat and Lucy is genuinely moving, poignant, hilarious (cue a mouse dropping from the ceiling), and ultimately compelling as Lonnie Hull DuPont experiences the sustaining power of love in furry form."

—**Susy Flory**, author or coauthor of eleven books, including *Thunder Dog*, a *New York Times* bestseller

"An engaging story of an accidental cat owner. Been there. The prose was so funny, touching and vivid, I felt like part of the family."

—**Dusty Rainbolt**, former president of Cat Writers Association and author of *Cat Scene Investigator: Solve Your Cat's Litter Box Mystery*

"My favorite glimpses of the holy come by way of thoughtful observance of the quotidian, honest sharing of a life, and simple, pure sentences—glimpses that come on little cat's feet, one might say. This delightful book is full of just those things."

—**Robert Benson**, author of *Between the Dreaming and the Coming True* and *Punching Holes in the Dark*

"If you love cats, don't miss this poignant book! Lonnie Hull DuPont has crafted an enchanting, heartwarming peek into the ways these delightful—and therapeutic—creatures enrich and teach their humans. Highly recommended!"

—**Erin Taylor Young**, author of *Surviving Henry* and cofounder of Write from the Deep

"This memoir is like a good, honest friend who compels you to listen to the wisdom and wit she has to share. From the first page, I was hooked. Through this tender love story between the author, her husband, and their fur-babies, I was touched by Kit Kat's love for her family, Lucy's zest for life, and Lonnie and Joe's unending willingness to learn what's best for their kitties. DuPont weaves in poignant memories from her childhood, humor, and practical insights about cats. I couldn't stop reading and, by the end, felt like I had a new best friend."

—**Susan Logan-McCracken**, former editor of *Cat Fancy* magazine and award-winning author

Books Compiled as Callie Smith Grant

The Cat on My Lap
The Cat in the Window
The Dog at My Feet
The Dog Next Door
The Horse of My Heart

Kit Kat and LUCY

THE COUNTRY CATS

Who Changed

A CITY GIRL'S WORLD

LONNIE HULL DuPONT

Revell

a division of Baker Publishing Group
Grand Rapids, Michigan

Published by Revell
a division of Baker Publishing Group
P.O. Box 6287, Grand Rapids, MI 49516-6287
www.revellbooks.com

Printed in the United States of America

Library of Congress Cataloging-in-Publication Data
Names: DuPont, Lonnie Hull, author.
Title: Kit Kat and Lucy : the country cats who changed a city girl's world / Lonnie Hull DuPont.
Description: Grand Rapids : Revell, 2016.
Identifiers: LCCN 2016016241 | ISBN 9780800727321 (pbk.)
Subjects: LCSH: DuPont, Lonnie Hull. | Cat owners—Religious life. | Cats—Religious aspects—Christianity. | Human-animal relationships—Religious aspects—Christianity. | Kit Kat (Cat) | Lucy (Cat)
Classification: LCC BV4596.A54 D8 2016 | DDC 818/.603 [B] —dc23
LC record available at https://lccn.loc.gov/2016016241

Some names and details have been changed to protect the privacy of the individuals involved.

16 17 18 19 20 21 22   7 6 5 4 3 2 1

In keeping with biblical principles of creation stewardship, Baker Publishing Group advocates the responsible use of our natural resources. As a member of the Green Press Initiative, our company uses recycled paper when possible. The text paper of this book is composed in part of post-consumer waste.

. . .

I dedicate this book...

To the memory of my extraordinary father-in-law and fellow lover of books, John (Jack) J. DuPont. I miss you, and I wish I could have handed this book to you.

To my lovely mother-in-law and fellow Cat Woman, Joan M. DuPont. You have treated me like one of your own from the moment we met, and I love you.

To my smart and spirited siblings-in-law—John DuPont, Cathy Tretheway, Jim DuPont, Robert DuPont, Ann-Marie DuPont, and Daniel DuPont. And to my very cool fellow "out-laws"—Jill DuPont, Earl Tretheway, and Joey DuPont. You are all so witty, so interesting, and so much fun. I love any chance to be with each and all of you.

And especially to my wonderful husband, Joe DuPont, who travels this road with me and never fails to make me laugh. I am so grateful for your unwavering love and support. Although the song says people leave their hearts in San Francisco, I found mine there and got to take it with me—thanks to you.

. . .

Contents

PROLOGUE

There are only two ways to live your life.
One is as though nothing is a miracle.
The other is as though everything is a
miracle.

Albert Einstein

When I was a single woman in my thirties, I lived in the heart of San Francisco. I loved it there. I stayed for ten years in a third-floor walk-up on Telegraph Hill, and I planned to live there forever.

This was the North Beach district, a handsome and historic Italian neighborhood, flanked by Chinatown and the Bay. I woke each morning to the sounds of foghorns and sea lions, to the smells of garlic and coffee, to a view outside my windows that included cable cars clanging toward downtown at their usual pace of nine miles per hour. My shower had a head-level window through which I could see all of the east side of Russian Hill bathed in morning gold. As I washed my hair, I watched the fog roll off the hill.

Every day I swam in an outdoor pool in my apartment complex—yes, right in the heart of the city. I walked everywhere I wanted to go, up and down those famous hills, on knees still young and strong. I was a poet who gained some local reputation in that mecca for poets. I made interesting, lifelong friends. I felt I had found my true home.

At the time, I worked as an acquisitions editor for a publishing house that specialized in books on religion and philosophy. Committee meetings where we decided what to publish were always lively, although often in these meetings we didn't necessarily know much about one another's area of expertise. One of the editors at these meetings presented projects in an area I didn't understand and even thought was a little weird. To be honest, I seldom had a clue what he was talking about, though he certainly was passionate about it, and I'm ashamed to admit I often mentally zoned out during his presentations.

One day as he presented with his usual intensity, I had begun making a mental grocery list—until the editor said something that broke through and caused me to look straight at him. I don't recall the context, but he said, "We've lost our connection to the land. We've lost our connection to the animals."

For me, this statement was startling and true. I recognized its truth in my heart immediately. I actually started to ache inside as I sat in that conference room. I *had* lost my connection to the land. I had especially lost my connection to the animals. I didn't realize until that moment how much I missed having animals in my life.

I was raised in rural southern Michigan on what had been the family farm. My ancestors homesteaded it in 1835, and we lived in the very house they built—my mother was born in front of the fireplace, and my nephew and his family live there today. I used to sleep by a corner window in my bedroom, tucked into the weather you might say, often waking up on summer nights to lightning storms or on winter mornings to ice frozen on the glass. We no longer had livestock and crops on the property, but we did have horses and large gardens of vegetables.

My playgrounds were old, ghostly, broken-down barns, an aging orchard, fields of tall grass, and stands of straight black locust trees planted by my great-grandfather for making no-longer-needed fence posts. For extra money, my sister and I grew vegetables to sell in a roadside stand, or we worked in the fields for local farmers. Beyond our family land, I had walked, ridden horses, or bicycled over much of this rural county before I could drive. I knew the land and felt connected to it.

I especially felt connected to the animals. There were few children within walking distance, so my friends were animals. As a child, I used to sing to the cows next door—a curious, attentive, and polite audience if ever there was one. We had at various times at our place horses and ponies, rabbits, and a stray rooster. There was a family dog in the house with no strong alpha—he had an obsessive-compulsive issue before we knew the term, but still was everybody's friend. And we had a succession of cats who usually chose me as their bond. The cats were my best friends of all.

I have strong memories of watching the night shadows of horses and deer grazing together outside my corner window.

I particularly remember this because at around age six or seven, I developed an anxiety problem. This resulted in constant, teeth-grinding worry punctuated by flare-ups of panic during the day and insomnia at night. Connecting with my cats soothed me more than anything, although I obsessed over their well-being. At bedtime, watching and listening to the wildlife outside my corner window helped me get through bad nights. It also helped when the family dog snored on the floor of my room. And there was always a cat on my bed.

I continued to have pets as a young adult in Michigan—a girl who couldn't figure out for the longest time what she wanted to be when she grew up. When I finally got serious about finishing college, I knew I'd have to move to another town. I gave away the last pet I would have for the next two decades, a sweet mixed-breed shepherd. I met her after she had given birth to eight puppies under my rented house. I found homes for the puppies but kept the momma, and she went everywhere with me for about a year. Since I was learning German at the time, I named her Freunde. You could say that she became bilingual, at least to the extent that I could speak commands and sweet nothings to her in my unimpressive German. *"Freunde, wo bist du?"*

Giving my dog away just about killed me, and I vowed I would never again have a pet until I was settled down, whatever that meant. That's how it was for the next twenty-plus years. I simply shut down inside about animals. I found other ways to handle my anxiety or I simply worked around it. I moved to Athens, Greece; New York City; San Francisco—and this country mouse rather happily turned into a city rat. I kept myself footloose and without ties for years, always able to move on when my work required it. I observed other people's pets but shoved down any longing to have them myself.

We've lost our connection to the land. We've lost our connection to the animals.

Let's go back to that publisher's meeting. If you had told me that day that in seven years I would be living back in rural Michigan with a husband and nary a coffeehouse within twenty-five miles, that we would be occupying an old farmhouse on a huge flat plain, and that I would be writing stories about animals, I'd have said, "Absolutely not."

Of course I had no way of knowing the future. A few years after that publisher's meeting, I met my husband Joe around the corner from my apartment. We had a whirlwind courtship. We began dating in September, and we fell in love around Thanksgiving. On bended knee, he asked me to marry him just before Christmas, and at the end of January, we were married on a rooftop in North Beach, surrounded by immediate family.

Joe moved into my apartment near the North Beach intersection of Grant and Vallejo where we had met and subsequently married. We were very happy with each other and happy with our home. We met a little late in life, so we would not be having children. We had a vague hope to have a dog someday and name it Elvis. Cats were out of the question because Joe was highly allergic to them.

We had a few blissful years, but then I lost a good job. I did freelance editorial work for a couple of years, but it became harder for the two of us to make enough money to support living in the increasingly more expensive city of San Francisco. We had no hope of owning a house there.

In addition to our financial situation, which was becoming hand-to-mouth rather quickly, my parents in Michigan were aging and having health crises. The day we found ourselves charging the rent to our credit card, Joe and I made a difficult decision.

A few weeks later, we packed our Geo Metro, drove over the Bay Bridge, and headed east across America to start over.

· 1 ·

A HOUSE AND A CAT

You will always be lucky if you know how
to make friends with strange cats.

Colonial American Proverb

To say moving from San Francisco to rural Michigan was
not easy for me would be an understatement. The moving
company said it well when they charged us half-price because
we were moving the wrong way at the wrong time—from
California to Michigan in late December. I cried as we drove
out of North Beach and past Chinatown, headed for the
Bay Bridge. A chain-link fence along Columbus Avenue was
stuffed with bok choy drying in the breeze, and it felt to me
like hundreds of little flags waving good-bye.

After the long trip, we moved into a flat in Ann Arbor
where Joe got a job with the University of Michigan and

I continued what I'd been doing the last couple of years—freelance editing and writing. We were there for nine months, a reluctant gestation period for merging into a new—or for me, old—state together. Ann Arbor's a nice city—I'd lived there before—and I would not have believed I could have a bad living experience there.

But on our street, the city was pulling down houses to make parking lots. To have handsome old houses and mature trees and even lilac bushes coming down around me in droves was depressing. Jackhammers ran all summer outside my windows. We never completely unpacked in those nine months.

One Saturday on a stunning late-September day, we were visiting the Jackson County Family Farm Day. This particular year, my brother-in-law's longhorn ranch was on the program, so Joe and I hung out in the hay barns with the kids and the steers and the cider and doughnuts. My folks were there too, and this was when my mother told me about a house several miles from the ranch. "I know you don't want to live out here," she said, "but you should see the house your brother-in-law bought. It just looks like you." She used that expression often—"It just looks like you"—when referring to anything that seemed to be to my taste. She was usually correct.

My brother-in-law had bought an eighty-acre farm on US-12, the oldest state highway in Michigan, in a county that was historic to the point of ghostly. He wanted the land, but he didn't want the house. It was for sale with about an acre. Since it was such a lovely day, Joe and I left the festivities and took a drive to find the house. Directions? Drive to the village of Moscow, head west for a couple of miles, look for a huge silo standing by itself on the left, then see a two-story brick house with a "for sale" sign. Address? Nobody remembered.

Off we went, and those minimal directions were perfect. The silo part had me worried, since a lone silo in rural Michigan is not exactly rare. But there stood the square brick house with a "for sale" sign. The first thing I noticed was that this was a very old house for Michigan. That part of the state was not settled until the late 1820s, around twenty-five years later than neighboring Ohio, and this clearly was a mid-nineteenth-century house. And a handsome one at that.

The next thing I noticed were the trees—seven huge maples, each of them four stories high, protecting the west and north sides of the house. And windows. So many of them. We pulled into the driveway and got out to see what we could see. We peered into the empty house through long, double-hung windows. They appeared to hold the original wavy glass, topped with what vintage architecture calls "eyebrows" over the frames. We walked around the house and counted twenty-seven of those windows.

"I'll bet this house isn't locked," I said to Joe.

"You're kidding." The trusting ways of country people never ceased to amaze my city-boy husband.

Everyone in farm country goes to the back door of a house, and so did we—and sure enough, the back doors were unlocked. We walked into an enclosed porch that led to a shabby mudroom, and beyond that all I could see was space. I hurried into that next room and found myself in the biggest farmhouse kitchen I have ever been in. I was immediately drawn to the east windows bathing the room in light.

This house is mine.

Whoa. Had I said that out loud? I heard it so plainly. But no, it apparently simply popped up in my mind.

Either way, I believed it.

We may have been nuts to buy a house at this particular time in our lives. We had good credit but no money. The house was so far from Joe's job that the commute would be an hour and fifteen minutes each way, half of it on two-lane country roads. I would be in the middle of nowhere by myself every day, all day, without a car, in a rural county where the only diversity was one thousand Amish residents. It didn't help that it was not far from where I grew up; I had had good reasons for leaving home years ago.

But I loved this house immediately, and so did Joe. No matter that it was 3,200 square feet for two people who had always lived in one-bedroom apartments. No matter that it needed work that neither of us knew how to do. My brother-in-law made a deal for us to rent for the first year, and within a matter of weeks, we moved in.

The first night we spent there, Joe reached for my hand. "Come outside with me," he said, "and let's look at our house."

It was a moonlit night in late October. We strolled around that big brick tank in the crisp autumn air, feeling like little kids who just got something cool for Christmas. The lamplight in the windows made the otherwise dark house seem to pulsate with life.

Would this mean I could say I'd settled down?

Could I have animals in my life again?

Would we get that dog named Elvis?

We had a short but snowy winter that first year. Oddly, it didn't snow until December and it never snowed again after February—not the winters I recalled from childhood. But it was very cold. We adjusted to the season. We taped up windows upstairs where snow came in. We unpacked slowly. We pulled up the avocado-green carpeting to expose glorious golden hardwood floors.

I spent a lot of time alone that first dark winter, and many evenings I waited anxiously as Joe made the long commute home. I'd putter around the rambling house and watch the lights of the semi-trucks flash by on our state road, sick to my stomach until I saw our Geo Metro turn into the driveway. The anxiety I felt was strong and familiar. I grew up with similar feelings and had handled them silently. Over the years, I'd learned to work around anxiety without medication. I didn't know I had an issue with a name. I thought something was simply wrong with me and always would be.

I do not know what exactly happened to change me into such an anxious child, growing up to be an anxious adult. Perhaps it was a perfect storm of my father's violent temper, my parents divorcing when I was four, both parents remarrying the following year, and my functioning in the aftermath of all that chaos. After the remarriages, my sister and I spent most weekends at our dad's house in the city. His new wife, my stepmother, was a nice, smiling woman; she and I would eventually become very close right up until her death in her eighties. But when I was a child, I don't remember seeing her or Dad around very much. We were left alone a lot. We kids would circle up with our cousins and a stepsister and spend days running around downtown Jackson. If it was cold out, we spent whole afternoons in movie theaters. I was the youngest and therefore sometimes not invited to go with them, so I spent many days even as a child wandering around the city of Jackson by myself.

I never liked going to Dad's house. I cannot think of a time

I wanted to go there. I wanted to be home with my mother and my animals and my own bed, but these were the days when children were not asked what they wanted. One thing that especially unnerved me at my father's house was that I never knew where I would sleep. I may have been on the chenille couch in the living room. I may have been in a windowed porch on a mattress with no sheets; the streetlights behind venetian blinds poured patterns of light over me in stripes and I felt like I was caged. I may have been in my teenage stepsister's room while her friends walked in, flipping on the overhead light, talking as if I wasn't there, blasting music on their transistor radios. To this day I have a weird dread of overhead lights. I slept very little on the weekends at Dad's.

When I would return home, I was relieved. I was close to my mother, and my stepfather fortunately was a good man. But my mother and stepfather had problems, and nobody was talking about it. There was no fighting, but there was a lot of silent tension. Since nothing was being said, I worried over things I tried to figure out myself—correctly or not—by listening and watching.

During those years I worried excessively over the well-being of my cats. The farm mentality was that cats could not be kept indoors exclusively. My mother would say, "They're really wild animals, and it's wrong to coop them up." My stepfather would note that during the Depression, when people moved from empty farmhouse to empty farmhouse as his family did, everyone left behind their cats. "And their wicker chairs," my mother would add.

So our cats were indoor-outdoor pets, letting themselves in and out of the house by the convenient way of a broken basement window with vines over it. My stepfather left it like that. Not a bad life for cats. But absolute misery for me if they didn't come home at night. Or were away for days, coming home beat up. Or never returned.

At any rate, now in the countryside of Moscow, Michigan, so many years later, it was like I was dropped right into the middle of the word *anxiety* once again. At least I lived in my own house and had control over my own living situation. In the past couple of decades, I had been able to distract myself from worrying most of the time. But now I simply could not, and I wasn't sure what to do about it. So I watched and waited.

The smell of spring in damp air showed up early after that first winter in the house. Then came a certain March evening. It rained softly outside and had just fallen dark. We lived on the first floor only at that time, our bedroom being one of the front rooms. As Joe and I readied for bed, I heard something I didn't want to hear—a cat crying outside. Close.

I looked out the sidelight windows of the front door, and there in a pool of light from our window sat a skinny, dark-colored kitten, about six or seven months old. She was all mouth, crying for food, and she was, as my late Oklahoma friend used to say, "homely as homemade sin."

Joe joined me at the window. The kitten continued to cry—she was incredibly loud—and seemed to look us right in the eye. I was distressed to see her. I knew we couldn't bring her inside because Joe was allergic, congested the minute we stepped into any house with cats. But it was obvious we would need to help this little creature out.

"We have to feed her," I said, "and *you* have to do it. I don't want to get attached to a cat that's eventually going to be killed by a truck."

"Don't worry," Joe said. "I can't get attached to something I'm allergic to."

Famous last words.

The first night, Joe took a dish of tuna fish out to one of the barns, and the kitten followed him. When Joe placed the dish on the ground, the kitten approached and drooled right on the ground. But before eating, she rubbed on Joe. She wove in and around his legs, purring, for quite some time. Joe, who was not used to cat behavior, felt he was being thanked. Such manners hooked my courteous husband right away.

We started buying cat food for the kitten after that. Every morning and every evening, Joe would tap a can on the side of a metal building and call for the kitten. She would appear and do that thing cats do, the winding, halting yet graceful waltz they make to get to your side. Then she rubbed on Joe's legs for a while, back and forth, dancing a circle eight on her black toes.

Joe the Allergic One would then pick the cat up and place her forehead against his and let her body dangle while he talked to her. Then he'd put her in front of her food and pet her back really hard while she ate. She loved it. It seemed as if she knew another creature was literally watching her back so she could eat in peace. Needless to say, Joe and the kitten bonded. We started calling her The Kitty. Actual naming meant claiming, after all, and this seemed safer.

Over the next few weeks, Joe continued feeding The Kitty, and we talked often about her future. We had no shelter for her other than the house, which she never asked to enter. We did not own the barns, and they were locked. Every now and then another stray would show up for food, and The Kitty hissed away every one of them—all of them bigger—until she had finished eating. Those strays never lasted long on the busy road. She, however, did. We had tremendous respect for her tough will. Her survival skills were superior. But Joe and I knew that even she would be no match for the trucks, coyotes, rifles, and Michigan winter where we lived.

My brother-in-law's longhorn ranch was about eight miles away. He offered to take The Kitty to be a mouser in the barns. That seemed like a safe enough life for the young cat—warm hay and regular meals and people around during the day, and it was on a road with less traffic than ours. Joe and I both felt that rehoming her was the right thing to do.

We waited one night for The Kitty to come to the back yard and cry for food. When she did, we put her in a box and hurried her into the car. I mentioned to Joe that she seemed a little round and might be pregnant, but I wasn't sure she was old enough to be. We knew nothing then of the practice of trap, neuter, and release for feral cats. We had so much to learn. I wasn't concerned at the time because if she did have a litter, they would be barn cats.

The kitten was very upset to be in the box, and she was mighty vocal about it. Eventually we would learn that, unlike most cats, she simply could not tolerate being in a box or a bag. The first time I would ever put a paper bag on the floor for her to play with, she would step around it without even looking at it. She had, as they say, issues.

That night, however, the box was all we had for her transport. We talked soothingly to her on the way to the ranch, but she cried the whole eight miles. It was a long drive for all of us. When we arrived, we took the box into the barn and opened it. The Kitty peeked out with what looked like terror in her eyes. She crawled over the edge, then, keeping low to the ground, she shot out of the barn into the night.

I was horrified. Her fear had been painful to observe, and now I was sure we'd never see her again. All my childhood anxiety about my cats' disappearances came scrambling to the surface.

But my calm husband—the cat's pair-bond—walked into the night and called. Sure enough, she had circled the barn and sat silhouetted in the distance. She made her way to Joe, and he picked her up. He took her back inside, communed with her forehead-to-forehead for a bit, then set her in front of her food and water. He stroked her back while she ate. Then we left.

As we drove away, Joe reminded me that we were doing the best thing. The cat wanted to live, and we wanted to help her live. Objectively I had to agree. But I felt we'd abandoned her. I was sick to my stomach all the way home.

In the next few days, I asked about The Kitty. My niece said she saw her once and never again.

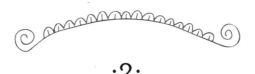

·2·

THE JOURNEY

There are no ordinary cats.

Colette

My work as a freelance editor and writer continued through our moves from San Francisco to Ann Arbor, then from Ann Arbor to Moscow. I set up my office in the mudroom of the house, which had some built-in shelving I could use. A south-facing window brought in just enough natural light. I got into a routine fairly quickly. A morning person, I rose early, made coffee, put in some personal writing, then woke Joe up with his coffee. He would be away for work usually around twelve hours per day—from a little before seven to a little after seven. If I was absorbed in a project, that was fine. But after city life, rambling around in that big house by myself all day felt odd. I was used to being around people. I was used to a quicker pace and more daily interactions and stimulation.

For the first few months, we had one car, the blue Geo Metro we drove from California, and it was gone all day with Joe. So we bought a car for me—another Geo Metro, a used, white, two-door 1990 stick shift that felt like driving a golf cart. No radio. No air-conditioning. But I liked it. The car was cheap enough that we had the cash to pay for it, and now when I needed to be around people, I could drive somewhere and read manuscripts. I had walked to coffeehouses in North Beach. Now I needed to find places where I could read in Moscow.

The closest place to get coffee near us was about five miles down the road—a truck stop that everyone knew by name, although there was no name on the building or on the sign. There was only a towering pole in the gravel parking lot with the word *EAT* on top, which Joe and I always thought looked like the word *FAT*. Inside were locals—farmers, truck drivers, and retirees—and even though I myself had waited tables in truck stops and diners in my younger years, it was disconcerting that every time I walked into this place, people literally stopped talking and watched me. I didn't think I looked like such a stranger, but apparently I did.

When I hauled out a 300-page manuscript to read (this predates using electronics for reading), the staring continued. California had outlawed smoking in restaurants several years before, but no such thing had happened in Michigan. I could ignore the unfriendly behavior by reading, but I was not used to being in smoke. So I gave up reading at the truck stop. I stayed home instead.

Although we were settling slowly but surely into what felt very much like our home, I was still feeling the aftereffects of moving cross-country, then moving again, lock, stock, and barrel, all within ten months. My anxiety got worse by the week. I would start out relatively happy in the morning, and as the day went on, I developed feelings of dread that surged up and down like ocean waves.

For some reason, these feelings especially raised their heads whenever I drove down the road toward my new home. There was a big sweeping S curve, and until I maneuvered that curve and could see my house standing on the plain in the distance, my adrenaline was up. I remembered having those feelings when I was younger—coming down the road I grew up on and feeling uneasy passing the thick woods until I could see the clearing where the family house stood. And the relief I felt that it was still standing.

During those young years, my feelings of uncertainty and fear focused on some horrible imaginary thing happening to my home or my mother or my cats. Terrifying scenarios whirled in my mind, and my adrenaline could stay up for a long time. If my mother and stepfather were out for the evening, I would sleep upstairs near my grandmother. I woke myself up several times a night, creeping down the stairs in the dark, to see if my mother was home. I would feel around in the blackness for the fur of her coat's collar or the tapestry of her evening bag. When I felt either of those things, I crept back up the stairs and finally slept.

Now again these many years later, that familiar anxiety was there, this time focused on something bad happening to Joe on his commute, something out of my control. I observed my feelings, kept them to myself, and went about my days, often sick to my stomach, hoping I would feel relief eventually.

One of the nicer things about moving near my family was that my relationship with my older sister picked up where it was years ago when we'd been very close. We could once again enjoy each other's company. Peg and her husband, Dick, worked their longhorn steer ranch where we rehomed The Kitty, and they lived in a house a few miles away from the ranch itself.

That first spring, calving was in full swing. There were going to be eighteen births, and Peg checked up often on the longhorn mommies-to-be. One humid day when I showed up at Peg's house, she said, "Get back in your car and follow me. One of the heifers is going to give birth today. I won't be able to stay, but you might want to watch."

We drove a few miles to a field and down a tractor lane to where we could see a big-bellied heifer off by herself in a large corral. She staggered back and forth, the front legs of her soon-to-be-born baby slowly inching out of her swaying body, then pulling partially back in, then back out. We stayed in our cars with the motors off so that we would not distract her in her labor. Not much more happened for a while, and eventually Peg waved at me and slowly drove off as planned.

I had nothing pressing to do, so I rolled down my window, settled down in my bucket seat, and waited. There was a light shower, and the fragrance of the rain and the wet earth mingled with earthier animal smells. I was glad that I could take all those odors; years of pitching horse manure in my youth had made it so.

After a while, the heifer lumbered over to a Quonset hut—

style metal shed that was open on both ends, allowing me visibility, though mostly in silhouette. The heifer lay down. She was down for only a few minutes, then she sprang back up. She lowered herself back down on her front legs to a kneeling position. She licked and nudged a dark form that didn't move.

I was a little concerned about that lack of movement at first. But then I was distracted by the most surprising sight: several longhorn cows with their young calves in tow were headed across the field toward the shed. They apparently had heard something I had not, and they were moving at a brisk clip. When they got to the shed, they queued up single file and, one by one, walked into the shed. They reached their noses down to sniff and nuzzle the newborn as they filed through.

I'm sure a rancher could tell me why they did this, but to my eyes, they were welcoming the new wee one to the world. The light rain continued, and the cows and calves sort of hovered around the outside of the shed. Eventually the mother nudged the little one's head up. I could see that all was well, and I drove back to my sister's house.

After a couple hours, I decided to see if the newborn was on his feet. I drove back to where he'd been born, and sure enough, there he was not far from the fence, standing on shaky legs, flanked by his mother and a longhorn auntie. He wasn't walking; he was still working on standing on those long wobbly legs. At one point, he sneezed and collapsed on the ground. It was awfully cute. Mother and Auntie watched him for a moment, then nosed him back up on his feet. Some of the umbilical cord was still hanging from his belly, and his mother leaned down and snagged it with the end of her horn. He staggered but managed to stay upright for that.

I continued to watch them until dusk. At some point, sitting there in the light spring rain with the engine off and my window down, I realized that I had not worried about anything in hours. I had been completely absorbed in the longhorns' world. For the first time in a long time, the pit of my stomach was completely relaxed. *We've lost our connection to the earth. We've lost our connection to the animals.* I drove home. When I maneuvered the S curve that night, I felt calm for the first time in months.

A few nights later, I was getting ready for bed. I was about to shut the front porch light off when I saw her. Our homely little kitten was sitting on the porch. It had been ten days since we'd left her at the ranch, and there she was, dirty and skinny again. The Kitty had somehow negotiated eight miles through farmland, swamps, and woods and across a busy highway to get back to us. Now she sat bathed in the porch light, looking at us through a sidelight window, her face and demeanor very quiet. She had unusual markings, so there was no doubt it was she. The little cat with the loud cries did not make a peep. She was simply too weary.

How on earth had she done it? We'd both heard of animals making such journeys—who hasn't?—but neither of us knew one personally. In fact, Joe was in such disbelief that he insisted my nephews had played a trick on us by bringing her back to our house. Knowing my nephews better than he did, I assured him that was not the case. Apparently The Kitty did not like living with the cattle at the ranch. Apparently she had determined that there had been some mistake, that our place was her home, and that she was simply going to have to go back there.

It took a few minutes of talking to each other and watching the kitten to get this figured out. Once we realized that the kitten really had walked back to us all by herself, we were tremendously impressed. And flattered. Joe and I looked at each other and said at the same time, "She stays." We opened the door and invited her inside. The kitten who would never before come near the house except to yowl for food and then skirt under the yew bushes waltzed right in and began rubbing on us.

"What about your allergy?" I asked Joe.

"I'll medicate," he said. "If she wants to be here that badly, she can be."

We fussed over her for a while. I fed her a can of tuna fish since we'd sent her food to the ranch, and then I petted her while she purred and rubbed on my legs. I picked her up for the first time, but that seemed to make her nervous. I put her back down.

Meanwhile, Joe sprinted out the door to race to the closest big box store. Once there, he had fifteen minutes before closing to lope through the place and get us cat-ready. Fortunately Joe is blessed with long legs. He came home with a litterbox and litter, food, and toys galore. We fed The Kitty some more and then played with her until she crawled under a cabinet where we couldn't reach her and fell sound asleep.

It was official. We had a cat.

The first couple of days with a feral cat in a house were tough. Once we committed to keeping her, we knew we couldn't let her outside, not with all the dangers. But we knew nothing about the wisdom of confining a cat to one small room while she adjusted to a new home. We simply closed our bedroom door that first night and let her prowl around the house to deal with her whereabouts at her own pace. The next morning, I found every item on our many wide windowsills knocked over. I also discovered that she had not used the litterbox, but she had relieved herself. Oh dear. We were going to have to deal with that somehow.

In the meantime, during Joe's late-night tear for cat paraphernalia, he had discovered an item called a Purr Pad, and he bought several of them for something like fifty cents apiece. The Purr Pad was a two-feet-square piece of coarse and nubby synthetic fabric, white in color. The first morning with our new cat, Joe placed a Purr Pad on the linoleum near her dishes. The cat parked herself on the Purr Pad and pretty much stayed there, grooming away the grime of her journey. The Purr Pad became so filthy from this that I replaced it with a fresh one by noon. Having been without cats for the past twenty years, I'd forgotten about their determination to be clean. I found watching her bathe to be soothing.

The Kitty seemed to appreciate the texture of the pad and probably a sense of personal space in 1,600 square feet of strange territory on that first floor, all of it open to her. For the first couple days, she would only stay in the kitchen on her Purr Pad or she would tuck herself under cabinets to watch the goings-on. She was okay with the kitchen linoleum, but carpeting and clutter seemed to make her nervous.

Unlike most cats, The Kitty did not take to the litterbox; it was, after all, a box, and she was not box-friendly. I was dismayed for about thirty-six hours over this turn of events. My childhood cats went outside for their business, so I really had no experience with handling this—or living with its repulsive odor. I scrubbed and scrubbed and worried.

But then Joe—her pair-bond—finally demonstrated for The Kitty, within reason, what needed to be done. He got down on his knees and scratched in the box with his fingers. The Kitty watched and listened. Joe saw her ears perk up, and he imagined a tiny bulb lighting up above her head—because he could see that she "got" it. She hopped in the box and did her appropriate thing immediately. She also learned to use a scratching post by watching Joe get on the floor and scratch at the new post himself. This was the first inkling I had that cats respond to modeling.

The Kitty now knew how to handle her needs, and she spent much of her days sleeping and grooming. I noticed then that she had some kind of healed injury that prevented her from grooming her right side past her shoulder. I didn't like to imagine how this happened. She certainly tried hard enough to groom the area, turning as hard as she could and licking the air, but was unable to connect with her fur. That would never improve.

We didn't name our new member of the family right away. Of course Elvis was out of the question. We both felt a name would come to us, that somehow the cat would name herself. And we waited for it to happen, though we did toss around a couple of possibilities. Batgirl rose to the top, because from behind, her head in silhouette looked like Batman. But it never seemed to stick.

One day in the kitchen where she liked to hang out, Joe made the suggestion that would stick. "What about Kit Kat? Like the clock. But spell it like the candy bar."

We both liked that kitschy vintage clock with its roving eyes and ticking tail. We had one in our kitchen in San Francisco, but the many small earthquakes California would experience made for shaky walls. Most residences and businesses in the older parts of the city were made of California redwood, which bounces in a quake. We'd often hear our windows and items on walls rattling in the night from low-level rumblings. Or sometimes from the late-Saturday-night appearances of the Hell's Angels motorcycle club roaring down Telegraph Hill. Such instability in the walls was not good for the Kit Cat clock. It would temporarily stop ticking. We would get it started again, but one day it simply stopped altogether.

But in the Moscow house, the brick walls were stable and unmoving. The previous Christmas we had each bought a Kit Cat clock for the other one. What a surprise when on Christmas morning we opened the same present from each other, which was as much fun as the actual present itself. We gave one clock away and kept the other. It now hung on the kitchen wall, where it ticked audibly and moved its eyes and black tail back and forth.

I liked the name. The kitten's strong personality caused her to twitch her tail a lot, much like the clock's wagging tail. And Kit Kat was kind of jazzy sounding for a cat whose fur had enough unusual markings to make an abstract painting. So Kit Kat it was.

I admit that when she was a youngster, Kit Kat was kind of odd-looking to me. But that's because I was not yet used to the unique beauty of a tortoiseshell cat. Mostly black with patches of cinnamon and honey, her unusual markings gave her an off-center look. Her upper eyelids were blonde, as if she were wearing pale eye shadow to contrast with her dark fur. One dot of blonde fur on her face was placed in a way that gave her a kind of feline beauty mark, *à la* Marilyn Monroe. Her eyes were round and hazel; her nose was black and slightly turned up. She was quite lovely.

And smart. Kit Kat learned her new name quickly, responding to it by rotating an ear. The day would arrive when she would come when called.

·3·

CAT MEN

A cat stretches from one end of my childhood to the other.

Blaga Dimitrova

Joe and I did a lot of things wrong at the beginning of our time with Kit Kat. As much as I loved cats, I learned that I didn't know that much about living with them 24/7. I hadn't had a cat in decades, and mine were always indoor-outdoor. And Joe had never had a cat of his own.

But once we committed to keeping the cat, we knew enough to take her as soon as possible to the vet to be spayed and to get her shots. That week I had a couple days of meetings a hundred miles away, so on Joe's way to work, he took Kit Kat to the vet's in a cardboard carrying case. On this journey to the vet's for the first time, Kit Kat let it be known how she felt about it all; she soaked the cardboard box through with urine. From that day forward, Joe's front passenger seat, no matter what he used to clean it, was never the same. And Kit Kat would never like to travel.

We left her at the vet's for the day for surgery and shots. That evening, I drove in from my meetings and met Joe (with a new sturdy carrier) at the vet's to take our Kit Kat home. I had chosen a clinic in Jackson, half an hour away from us, because decades ago they had treated my Freunde when I shut her foot in the car door. I had raced to the closest vet that awful day, sobbing the whole time. Meanwhile my sweet dog stopped crying herself and began licking my face as if to tell me it would all be fine. When I carried her inside the clinic, so choked up I could barely speak, they had taken her from me immediately and treated me very kindly. That story had a happy ending.

Not so much this time. Joe and I met at this same vet's office—a much larger operation now—to pick up our cat. But we faced very bad news. Kit Kat was going to die, they said—and soon. During the spaying, the vets saw inside Kit Kat an advanced case of feline infectious peritonitis (FIP). They said she was in what they called "the wet stages" of FIP, and this is always fatal. Although she was currently asymptomatic, she wouldn't live another year, not even close to it. They offered to euthanize her.

Before I had a chance to react, Joe said, "Absolutely not. We'll take her home. Just tell us what to expect." So we were given a quick education on FIP, again reminded that she was not going to live long.

"When the time comes," said Joe, "is there anything we can do to euthanize her at home?"

"You could take her out and shoot her," the vet said with a shrug, "but that's about all."

Joe stared at the vet, properly horrified.

Welcome home, I said to myself.

We would be changing vets.

Back at the house, Joe and I placed Kit Kat on the bed, petted her, and discussed our situation. We had always respected her, and we had grown very fond of her. Much like Kit Kat had decided she belonged to us, we felt that we belonged to her as well. So we decided we would give her a happy home for the rest of her life, no matter how brief that might be.

That night, with a terminal diagnosis, stitches in her belly from spaying, and a fresh mani-pedi, Miss Kit Kat caught a mouse. Its corpse lay next to Kit Kat's Purr Pad in the morning. We were pleased. It seemed to be evidence of our cat's resilience and determination to survive. From then on, we worked at putting her disease out of our minds. Instead, we treated her as if she would be with us for a long time.

Once Kit Kat adjusted to living indoors with a litterbox, she turned out to be a model house cat. She didn't get on the kitchen table or counters (not that we ever saw anyway), she didn't chew on the houseplants, and she loved guests. The homely little kitten with the strange markings grew into a sleek, shockingly handsome tortoiseshell—mostly black with flecks of gold and cinnamon and a golden belly. She was very good company—a pleasure to have around. She had had to grow up early, and very little kitten spirit remained, so she rarely played. When she did play, it seemed like she didn't know it was a game. She seemed to understand there was a goal in what she was doing, and once the goal was accomplished, her work was done; she simply walked away from the toy.

Given the bonding Joe and Kit Kat had developed outdoors, she would to some extent always be Joe's cat. But she pulled me into her charms too. At first she was not a lap cat at all. She seemed to be one of those four-on-the-floor cats who did not want to be held. I wanted to be able to handle my cat like I did my childhood cats, whom I used to carry around draped over my shoulder. Kit Kat, however, did not encourage that.

One day soon after Kit Kat moved indoors, I wasn't feeling well and decided to take a nap midday. As I dozed off, I saw Kit Kat join me on the bed and curl up near my head. When I woke up, I was lying on my right side, and something was pressed against my right eye. I slowly opened my left eye and saw the profile of a black turned-up nose in my line of vision. Kit Kat's little head was tucked up against my right eye socket, and I could only see the silhouette of her face and nose. She had moved closer to me and snuggled right up to my face.

Maybe that cautious little cat finally felt safe enough to sleep pressed against a human. Or maybe this was her feline way of helping me when I wasn't feeling up to snuff. Whatever the case, I fell even more in love with my girl right then.

This physical contact was a sneak peek at things to come. Kit Kat would eventually very much like to be held and rocked. She would climb on me, flex her paws into me, and purr, eyes glassy. She became so cuddly that sometimes I felt as if I had a living teddy bear; her fur even smelled like a plush toy to me. The day would come when any time either

Joe or I took a nap, we would take Kit Kat along and put her in the bed with us. There she curled on her side, placed her head between our pillows, and allowed us to tuck the covers under her chin. Eventually she had her own small pillow that we placed between ours.

Kit Kat's devotion to Joe was especially touching. Since Joe would get down on the floor and interact with her, we wondered if she thought he was a fellow cat. She stayed in his presence when he was home, literally following him from room to room. She rubbed and rubbed on his pant legs. She groomed his hair when he lay down for a nap. He had been her savior, and she adored him.

Each weekday Kit Kat waited for Joe to come home from work by facing the direction of the door she knew he would walk through. She would start that vigilance at about 6:00 p.m. Since I had already been doing that out of anxiety, it was almost as if she shouldered the worry for me, and I could instead focus on her. If I was holding her when Joe unlocked the back door, Kit Kat would snap to attention, dive off my lap, and reach him before the back door closed. For the rest of the evening, I was pretty much chopped liver. She only had eyes for Joe.

This was the second time I would live with a cat who favored the man of the house.

Boots was my feline companion from my early teens until I moved out of my mother's house at age eighteen. She helped me limp through adolescence, and best of all, she served as a feline liaison between my initially distant stepfather and me.

I had had a run of bad luck when I was a child with two of my cats, each of them a stray, each named Fluffy. The first

Fluffy was a beautiful longhaired gray with a charming disposition. I don't recall other members of the family paying
much attention to her, but she was certainly my friend. Fluffy
let me drape her over my shoulder and carry her everywhere.
She slept at the foot of my bed every night.

I was ten years old when President John F. Kennedy was
assassinated. I hurried home from school early that day, as did
schoolchildren all over a frightened nation. At home, I found
Fluffy stretched out in the middle of the living room floor
and clearly not well. I spent the weekend lying on the floor
with her, worrying, or watching the television coverage of the
assassination, including seeing Jack Ruby shoot Lee Harvey
Oswald on live TV. I was sick to my stomach most of the time.

The country was in mourning all that weekend in a way we
don't see today. Commerce shut down until after the funeral,
and that included veterinarians' offices. As Fluffy worsened,
Mom promised we'd take her to the vet's after the weekend.
Since in those days nobody in the farmland where I lived
would ever have considered a sick cat an emergency, this
meant we could not take Fluffy to the vet until after the president's funeral on Monday. After the funeral, however, was
too late, and Fluffy died at the vet's office during the night.
The tension of the nation—and of my house—compounded
my devastation.

I spent that winter without a cat on my bed. Then the
following spring, while walking home from school, I was
approached by another longhaired gray cat on the side of
the road. She looked so much like Fluffy that I did a double
take. I'd never seen this cat before. She simply walked out
of a grassy ditch, gave a friendly meow, and rubbed around
my ankles in a figure eight.

I bent down to pet the gray cat. She was comfortable with me, and I assumed she was a drop-off. When I started walking again, she followed me home. My mother gently asked me if I had "helped" the cat come home with me. But I was much too sensitive a child to have lured home someone else's pet. The cat followed me that day of her own volition, and she chose to stay. I believed God sent me this beautiful clone of Fluffy—I still believe that—to help me through my worries. I was tremendously grateful for her.

While the first Fluffy was a sweet creature, this Fluffy was even sweeter. She, too, liked to be placed over my shoulder and carried everywhere. Fluffy #2 and our palomino gelding adored each other in a way I'd never seen between cat and horse. If I wanted to ride but the horse didn't want to be saddled, I would place Fluffy on my shoulder and walk into the grazing field. "Look who I have," I would coo to the horse.

The palomino would raise his head and saunter over. Fluffy purred while the horse nuzzled her. Then as I walked to the barn, the palomino followed the purring Fluffy. I would plop Fluffy in the manger so the horse could nuzzle her, and he allowed himself to be saddled without so much as a whinny. He even liked me to lay Fluffy across his back while he grazed, something that should have been dangerous. He'd turn his head and nuzzle Fluffy—who purred the entire time—then go back to grazing.

Fluffy #2 and I had a couple of good years together. Then she disappeared one day and never returned. After my panicky calls to her night after night, it slowly became clear she wasn't ever coming back. I was so inconsolable that at Christmas that year, my mother promised we would be intentional about finding another cat after the new year. For weeks, I rose before everyone else in the morning to pore over the pet section of the classified ads, looking for another cat. Eventually I found an ad in which a woman wanted a home for what she called her "favorite cat."

Mom called the woman and learned that this cat needed more attention than the woman could give her because of her other house cats. When Mom told her the cat would be for a twelve-year-old, the woman responded that her cat was not used to children. I heard my mother say, "My daughter is very mature for her age." Apparently that was good enough. Or maybe it was hard to find a home for an adult cat who possessed a mighty strong will.

Mom and I drove to the lady's house that night, and we could see right away why Favorite Cat needed more attention. There were eighteen cats living in that small bungalow, and it was a sight I'd never seen before and never forgot. They were all hanging out in a cramped dining room, and the animal energy was noisy and intense. Cats vocalized and crawled all over the tops of tables and old-fashioned buffets. It felt like we were interlopers in a miniature house of cats at the zoo.

Boots, already named, strolled into the room. She was a handsome, sturdy cat of about three years, with round and expressive green eyes. Her short-haired coat was slate gray with white markings on her face and chest as well as on all her feet, creating perfect little boots. I would eventually learn that she was passionate, charming, and fierce. But at this first introduction, I simply noted her regal demeanor.

Boots must have caught on immediately that I was her ticket out of this feline frat house because she looked me straight in the eye, then pranced over and rubbed on me and only me. This greatly impressed the woman, who remarked to my mother that Boots usually didn't like children. I now wonder how many children had actually been inside the cat lady's house. At any rate, Boots became mine to take home.

Like the Fluffys before her, Boots slept on my bed every night and was a constant companion for me. Unlike the Fluffys, however, Boots was not what one would call sweet. She was not easygoing by any means, and she was certainly not going to be draped over my shoulder or even picked up. She made that clear immediately—right after she whipped the family dog into some kind of canine she could live with.

But I loved Boots right away, and she seemed to like me well enough. I talked to her all the time, and she seemed to listen, her lovely white paws placed primly together as she looked into my eyes with a wise and interested expression. This had not been the case with either Fluffy. I talked to Boots so much that one night I dreamed she could speak too. Her voice was high and queenly and pitched like tiny bells. As a child I read Edgar Allen Poe, and Boots' voice made me think of the word he invented to describe a certain ringing sound: *tintinnabulation*. I asked Boots in the dream why she'd never spoken before, and she simply laughed a sweet little laugh.

Since I was the person Boots slept with, this meant I was the one she woke up to get the day started. She did this by sitting on the nightstand and moving breakable items with her paw. The gentle scraping would wake me, and if I didn't get up, something would land on the floor. But it certainly beat alarm clocks.

And Boots had a way with my stepfather.

One morning during the early silent years before Boots, I had seen my stepfather—who I was now calling Dad—feed a stray cat at the back door. We were always firmly instructed by my mother not to feed any more strays. Mom had more pets than she wanted, and they were almost never chosen, so she could be a little shrill about the stray thing.

But here was tense, quiet Dad offering a bowl of milk to a strange cat at the door. Even better, he was speaking to it, softly and gently. I hadn't seen him talk to either Fluffy, so I wondered, *Is this really Dad?* In my world of stoic farmers and other hardworking men, I never saw a man pay positive attention to a cat. Never. To see the tough and usually silent Dad paying such sweet attention to a cat . . . well, this knocked me out. Dad raised his head and saw me. A look of guilt flashed across his face. "Don't tell your mother" was all he said.

Now I knew there was more to Dad than I realized. And it didn't take long after she moved in for Boots to discover the Inner Dad. She followed him around, prancing, purring, flirting, rubbing on his legs. And Dad liked it. He talked to her. He talked more to Boots than he talked to any of the humans in the house. He even sang to her. He made up corny little tunes with her name in them, and when he thought nobody was listening, he sang them to Boots.

In return, Boots sat with him while he had his very-early-morning coffee by himself in the dark kitchen. She slept on his lap when he read the paper and on his clothes when he was away at work. And then Boots became a link between Dad and me. How did she do that?

In a house where people don't speak much, one can start believing they aren't listening either. But apparently Dad was listening to me speak to Boots. I sometimes called Boots other nicknames, one being Mrs. Boogan. She was so stately that

I felt she seemed like a Mrs. Somebody, and Mrs. Boogan was the name that presented itself while I cooed over her. Pretty soon I heard Dad calling the cat Mrs. Boogan. After a while, that's all he called her. He even used her nickname in his silly songs.

When we sat at the silent supper table, sometimes Boots would hop up on an unoccupied chair and watch us eat for a bit. Eventually she would slowly extend one paw to the table. Either Dad or I would say in a mildly scolding tone, "Mrs. Boooogan . . ." She would stop her paw and flex it in midair and look around the table as if to say, "Is there a problem?" It was so charming that we all relaxed. We teased her and fussed over her, and she loved the limelight.

Boots became something Dad and I had in common. If we had been away, the first thing Dad or I would ask about upon returning home was Boots. We both kept an eye out for her. We both talked to her. And sometimes, we talked to each other through her. I came to believe that Boots soothed Dad's nerves—the word they used for anxiety back then—as much as she soothed mine.

Now these many years later, I had another "man's cat." Kit Kat adored the man of our house. She also had a similar temperament to my strong-willed Boots. Physically they were both full-bodied with round, expressive eyes. Both were passionate, intelligent, fierce—so much so that all those years after Boots, I found myself calling Kit Kat by Boots' name on occasion. I heard my mother do it too.

But let's go back to my stepdad and me. The day came when he and I could relax with one another. When I was old enough to drive, we had more to talk about. Years later I came to the conclusion that he was simply never comfortable with children, and as I grew older, we developed a bond. There came a day when we never lacked for something to talk about.

My tough, silent stepfather wept openly at my wedding. A few years after that, at the time he lay dying in Florida, I was dreaming about him in Tennessee. He told my mother that I was in the room, next to him.

We can thank our Boots for that connection.

·4·

MOTHERING

The ideal of calm exists in a sitting cat.

Jules Renard

There was something else going on in my life at the time of
Kit Kat's moving in.

My sister and I were each adopted at birth, three years
apart. I had always wanted to find my biological roots. When
I was nineteen, through a lot of searching, I discovered the
whereabouts of my birth mother. Her name was Elaine, and
she lived right in my hometown of Jackson.

I did not know exactly what to do with that information
at nineteen. Knocking on Elaine's front door and surprising her was out of the question. I wanted to meet her, but
I needed to be gentle about it, even more so when I learned

she'd had no other children. Since I couldn't decide what to do, I did nothing for many years.

A decade later, I moved to Greece for a year. Elaine was always on my mind, and now that I lived so far away, it seemed safe to contact her. I wrote a long letter to her on yellow legal paper, carefully worded so that she would know who I was but hopefully nobody else would. Without actually telling her that I was her daughter, I introduced myself with my birth date and the name she gave me when I was born—Patricia Jo. I told her that I respected and appreciated what she did, that I had wound up with people who loved me, and that I was living a good life. I assumed she would want to know this. I added some details about myself, and I asked if she might like to meet me when I returned stateside. Then I took a deep breath and sent the letter off.

I did not hear back.

A few years later when I moved to Queens, New York, I wrote her again. When I moved to San Francisco, I wrote to her two more times. She never answered my letters.

I gave this much consideration over the years. After being fairly sure she received my letters since none were returned, I came to believe that it was too painful for her to hear from me. She had been a single woman from a middle-class family. Giving birth to a baby out of wedlock in the 1950s had been a shameful situation for a young woman. She probably wasn't going to revisit that. I needed to stand down.

I wrote her one last brief letter. I told her as gently as I could that it was all right, I understood—she didn't need to know me, and I wouldn't write again. I would appreciate it, though, if she would send me any family medical history I should know. Having worked in the direct mail industry for a few years where we made responding as simple as possible, I included a medical history form from my doctor and a self-addressed stamped envelope.

Still nothing. Now I was certain that her hurt was too deep and the shame too strong. I felt I needed to leave her alone. So I did.

It became my habit every time I visited Michigan from California, however, to cruise by Elaine's house. It was a modest, two-story structure on a tree-lined street. Its front porch had been glassed in, and those windows had shelves that were cluttered with knickknacks, giving the porch an oddly walled-in look.

One night on my way to a dinner party, I did my drive-by in the dark, and for the first time, I saw her. She was sitting in the corner of the glassed-in porch, reading. The end of the porch didn't have shelves on the windows, so from that side of the house, I could see her clearly. There was a lamp shining over one shoulder, lighting up half her face, and she was wearing reading glasses. I had a picture of her I had cut from the newspaper years ago, and I could tell this was indeed my birth mother.

I couldn't pull myself away. I parked alongside the curb in front of the house next door and watched her for a long time. I got out of my car. I walked up the sidewalk of the house next door and stood in front of its stoop. In the dark, I knew nobody could see me—not the residents of that house, not Elaine. I was careful to stay outside a circle of light from a back porch lamp in the neighbor's yard. I stood in the dark for a long time and watched my birth mother read.

Then it was as if I could not contain myself—I stepped into the circle of porch light. A driveway and a glass wall separated me from the woman who gave me life. My adrenaline rushed as I stood there. The moment seemed to freeze in place. If she looked up, she would surely see me.

But she never looked up.

Eventually I retreated back into the dark. I watched her for a while longer from that safe spot, then I turned away, got in my car, and left. I never saw her again.

I could not know that on the very night we took Kit Kat to the longhorn ranch, Elaine died in Jackson. I found out three days later, when her friends tracked me down. In the decades of Elaine knowing these friends, she had never told them she'd had a child. They discovered it when they came across my letters—letters she had kept together all those years in a place next to the reading chair on the glassed-in porch.

The day after we brought Kit Kat home from the vet, I attended my birth mother's memorial service. I met Elaine's close friends and many of my biological relatives that day for the first time. They were all so happy to meet me and to have some semblance of their loved one remaining—the daughter most of them had not known about. One aunt took my hands with tears in her eyes and said, "God is so good!"

I learned at the memorial service that Elaine's confirmation verse had been "Make a joyful noise unto the Lord" and that she had a wonderful laugh. I learned she loved to sing. Her favorite song was "Mack the Knife," a detail I found particularly delightful for some reason. And I learned that, like me, Elaine was a voracious reader.

From that day on, I got to know more about Elaine through her friends and my new relatives. I was happy that I had at least this much. Perhaps only adopted people can really understand this, but at the age of forty-six, for the first time in my life I felt grounded.

Nevertheless, a new sadness was living inside me. I had always hoped that one day, Elaine and I would meet. I had figured there was still time. But it was not so. I was—and still am—terribly disappointed that never in this world would I meet the woman who gave birth to me.

My emotions flipped around, and for a while I felt oddly detached from any deep feeling about Elaine at all. In fact, I found there were times over the next year when I couldn't even bring myself to stay in contact with the new relatives and friends, and I didn't understand why.

At home, I found maternal feelings rising in me toward Kit Kat. I found myself holding Kit Kat, rocking her, and crying. Why? On the surface, I didn't want my terminally ill cat to die, and I felt protective. But on another level, I knew that she was the vehicle that might help me connect to my deeply buried grief about the woman who bore me but would not know me. Ever.

Kit Kat was accommodating to my weepiness. She would stay close by, purring her unique purr that sounded like a toy truck revving its engine. After a while she would jump down and go about her cat day. I'd feel better. And I'd go about my human day.

A few weeks after Elaine's memorial service, my new aunts asked if I wanted to see the house Elaine grew up in before they sold it. It turned out that she had been living in her childhood home—this was the house where I did my drive-bys, the house where I saw Elaine on the porch.

My aunts and I walked inside, upstairs, down into the

basement, then back up and through the length of the house on the ground floor. When we walked into the front bedroom, Elaine's younger sister pointed to the bare floor by the window. "Right there, Lonnie," she said. "Right there was a bed, and I watched Elaine while she was in labor with you. I was eight years old."

Standing in that room struck me surprisingly hard. Elaine had labored right there to deliver me into the world. She was young and single and afraid. I had lived with her in her womb for nine months in this very house. I had let her know in this room that I needed to be born.

My lifelong disembodied feelings about my birth suddenly took shape in front of me in that bedroom. I did not start to exist the day the county called my parents to ask if they wanted a baby girl. I existed long before, in Elaine's body, right here. When she—and I—left for the hospital that winter morning for my birth, I would not return with her.

It was powerful stuff. But I still could not grieve . . .

A wonderful thing happened by summer's end. Or rather, didn't happen. Kit Kat didn't get sick. Instead, she got husky and gorgeous. She was smart and quick, and she continued to live for Joe. She liked us to watch her while she ate. Sometimes if we left her alone for the day, she wouldn't eat until we came back and sat with her at her cat dish. We were well-trained.

Another wonderful thing happened. Joe had been taking drugs for his cat allergy. But after a few weeks of Kit Kat living with us, Joe's allergy disappeared. Now both my cat and my husband were healthier than they were supposed to be. Kit Kat slept on our bed every night.

One day I took Kit Kat back to the Jackson vet to get

her claws trimmed and an updated evaluation. I had not yet found another vet, and I planned on this being our last visit to this clinic. I drew a different vet this time.

"How do you think her FIP is?" I asked.

The vet looked at me, then back at Kit Kat. "This cat has FIP?" she asked. "Who told you that?"

I paused. "This clinic told me."

The vet looked a little perplexed. "Did they see it in wet stages when they spayed her?"

"Yes," I said. "Doesn't she have it?"

"Well," she drawled, "sometimes other things look like FIP. The fact that your cat has not gotten sick but also seems to be very healthy does make me wonder. I'm not saying she doesn't have it, but I'm not saying she does, either."

What does one do with that statement?

I've since learned that there is a blood test for FIP, but the vets didn't test Kit Kat. Maybe since she was a homely stray, they skipped a mighty big step. I don't know. But back when they'd diagnosed her, I didn't know there was a blood test. It would have taken a few days to get the results because the blood test would have been evaluated by Michigan State University's vet school. So these vets made the diagnosis strictly based on what they saw inside Kit Kat. Armed with the doctor's vague comments, I took my cat home with a flicker of hope in my heart, daring to believe that she might not die so soon.

After a round of veterinary visits, again without blood tests (she was six years old before a vet actually tested her), the general consensus was that there had been a misdiagnosis. One vet suggested that what had looked like wet stages of FIP may have been what was left over from a pregnancy in our young cat. I recalled my comment to Joe when we took Kit Kat to the ranch that she seemed fat and might be pregnant. When she came back to us, she was skinny, which I figured was from the journey and not enough access to food. I suppose she had time to have given birth while she was gone. But unless the kittens were stillborn (my first Fluffy had stillborn kittens she began giving birth to on my bed), it was unlikely Kit Kat would have abandoned a litter to come back to us. The maternal instinct in cats is fierce. Who can forget the New York City cat firefighters found moving her newborns out of an inferno one by one and suffering horrible burns herself in the process? Yet she kept going back in.

The happy bottom line seemed to be that we might get to keep this marvelous creature for a long time. One vet said, "If your cat had FIP, she'd be dead by now, and she certainly wouldn't be this hale and hearty."

There was also that other bonus: Joe had stopped blowing his nose. His cat allergy was gone, never to return.

Soon after I learned that Kit Kat likely did not have FIP, I had a dream about my birth mother. By now it had been six months since Elaine died, and I dreamed that I could visit her. I went up in a jet. Elaine entered the aircraft mid-flight from the back of the plane and walked down the aisle, beaming at me. She sat next to me and curled around me, never speaking, just smiling. I started talking to her. I told her all about myself, about my childhood, and about my love of books, a love I knew she shared in her life. She nodded and almost cooed, but she never spoke.

I felt so happy. I felt love radiate from her, and I felt something strongly maternal flow from her. I almost expected her to count my fingers and toes. I had the realization that in the next life, we get to be the individual God created each of us to be, before our walls go up and cloak parts of who we are, before we're burdened with fear and anxiety. I felt I was experiencing the real Elaine.

Eventually I understood that she had to leave. I stopped talking, and she quietly held my hand. Then she stood, walked back down the aisle, and disappeared.

When I woke up, I felt as though I had met Elaine as a three-dimensional person; the dream was that vivid. I was so very sorry she was never able to bring down her own walls enough to meet me while she was alive. I finally felt tremendous grief over this.

Kit Kat started climbing on my lap and kneading her paws into me. I felt her little claws and loved her and cried for all that was lost. Fortunately after a few weeks of this, my emotions settled down. My maternal feelings toward Kit Kat slowly relaxed, and my grief about my birth mother turned into the dull ache it needed to be.

Life moved on. Joe and I went about our lives, working our jobs and fixing up the old house and trying to find time to be together. We both fell more and more in love with the little creature who walked eight miles back to us—that ugly-duckling-turned-swan with the superior survival instincts and soulful personality, the little cat who let me mother her and then mothered me back, whose life seemed to be a series of small miracles, and who apparently loved us as much as we loved her.

·5·

KIT KAT

The cat is not a commonplace creature
when she loves.

M. Fee

Joe and I both have strong personalities. We know this about
ourselves, and it most likely has made our marriage more
interesting. But we were both humbled by the dawning reality that the strongest personality in our house was Kit Kat's.

How this cat got us to do exactly what she wanted us to
do amazed us. How she refused to do what she didn't want
to do was equally amazing. If she wanted us to follow her,
she indicated it by moving forward, pausing, and turning on
her toes to look over her shoulder to see if we were following—and we were. If she wanted to be held, she would rub
and rub or join us while we sat—and she would be held. If

she did not want to be picked up, she stayed on the move, just a couple feet ahead of us. At such times, even Joe's long legs were no competition for those four determined little cat legs. What was most amazing of all, however, was how this strong-willed creature knew when we weren't feeling up to par—and then how she helped us.

We gave our girl several titles: Kit Kat the Social Director (because she greeted guests at the door), Kit Kat the Killer (because we'd seen her hunting skills firsthand), and when we were not feeling well, she was Kit Kat the Comforter. She could get Joe to rest and relax in a way that was very sweet and effective. And she helped me with my anxiety.

How did a cat help me with my anxiety? It started with her insisting on being held and rocked when she first moved in with us as I grieved over my biological mother's death. Beyond that, many times over the years when I rose in the night, worrying over something and too anxious to get back to sleep, Kit Kat would leave the bed too. She would follow me, crawl on my lap, then stretch up to sprawl over my heart and purr into my left ear.

I don't know how she knew I was anxious, but her behavior led me to believe she did know. I am confident that if we took a blood pressure reading right then, mine would be sinking nicely; certainly there's research that would support that. I would hold Kit Kat close and squeeze her solid little body while she purred. After a while, I'd take us both back to bed, my anxiety under wraps.

There are Old World myths that the purrs of a tortoiseshell cat are healing. On those dark nights, I'd have had to agree.

It was a pleasure to have such a soulful and intelligent cat in the house. But one of Kit Kat's clearest characteristics at this point in her life was that she was highly anxious. It didn't pass my notice that an anxious feline had chosen to move in with me, an anxious human. She moved in with Joe, too, of course, but I spent more time with Kit Kat the Anxious. We learned to know each other's issues well.

I have a friend who named her stray cat Miss Scarlett, because, like our heroine from *Gone with the Wind*, when she realized she'd found a home, the cat seemed to have taken an oath that she'd never be hungry again. Such was the case with Kit Kat. She had a thing about food availability. All those months of begging and hunting for food out there in the wild did something to her, and it wasn't simply that she expressed tremendous interest in all things edible, which she did. I know animals live in the present, but Kit Kat seemed to dread the prospect of deprivation, and when it came to her food, she was highly insecure.

If the bottom of her ceramic food dish was not completely covered with dry food—that is, if any white showed at all— Kit Kat became anxious. She would look at it, look at us, prance around the dishes, rub around our ankles, and meow. If we were sleeping and had neglected to fill the food bowls before retiring, she was known to get me up in the middle of the night. Once her bowl was full, she would eat a little from it and relax. It seemed like she was checking to make sure her eyes didn't deceive her.

I was reminded of that wonderful book, *The Cat Who Came for Christmas*, in which author Cleveland Amory's rescued alley cat was also obsessed with having visible food on hand. Amory began keeping a packet of Tender Vittles next to his own bed. When the cat woke him in the middle of the night, Amory would roll over half asleep, rip open a packet of food, and dump it in a bowl on the floor, then go back to sleep. Every night.

I, however, preferred to have enough food in the bowl for my cat to get through the night—especially since Kit Kat never woke Joe up for food, only me. She did that by hopping all her fifteen pounds on top of me. How she seemed to know where my bladder was, I cannot imagine. Or sometimes she placed her paw on my face and very slowly, even gently, sank her claws into my skin until I was awake—and knew why I was awake.

Because of the food issue, we learned to board Kit Kat the night before a surgery. If she was not allowed to eat after midnight, nobody in the house was going to get any sleep. She became panicked and highly expressive about her empty food dish all night. There was pacing and there was crying. It took only one night of Kit Kat's food panic, followed by a morning of her looking at us as if to say, "Thank heavens you're up! Can't you see there's no *food*?" And the pacing and the crying would kick in again. This was too much. We learned it was best for all whenever Kit Kat had a surgery to bundle her up the night before with a towel that smelled like home and board her at the vet's.

Kit Kat's general anxiety morphed into fear about other things. She was frightened of loud noises, a fear that undoubtedly saved her life many a time on her hike back to our place. In the house, however, it was painful to watch her expressions of fear. Thunder, vacuum cleaners, the coffee-bean grinder, the popcorn popper, and even strange loud voices all sent our normally quiet and regal creature scurrying away to hide. We needed to learn how to live more deliberately with the fearful, feral cat who adopted us. And in retrospect, at first we were not always good cat guardians.

Shortly after Kit Kat first moved in, we had to have the house fumigated for fleas from a previous tenant's dog. It would take six hours, during which all living creatures needed to stay away from the house. We had a plan—take Kit Kat to my brother-in-law's barn out back where there was a glassed-in office, and we'd go visit friends. That made perfect sense to us.

We carried Kit Kat out of the house and across the yard to the barn. We settled her in the office with food and water and litterbox. We figured she'd enjoy the new smells and the window.

It was later on that we realized how wrong we were. We had treated her as if she were a dog who would wait obediently until we came back. But cats are not small dogs, and Kit Kat hated what we thought she'd like. Dogs are predators and approach their world in that way with a certain confidence. Cats, on the other hand, are both predator and prey, and we'd just left our cat exposed. We'd deprived her of all her safe and familiar smells and hiding places.

And it was the breaking of trust. Had the humans abandoned her—again?

Six hours later when we retrieved Kit Kat, the terrorized look on her face broke my heart. We took her back into the house and watched her cautiously re-acclimate to her own abode, her own sleeping areas, her food dishes, everything familiar. She crept around, low to the ground, checking things out, cocking her ear for potential danger. We came to realize that our lack of cat knowledge caused our anxious cat even more anxiety. We knew we could never again take her to a strange place (aside from the vet) and leave her without us. At home, she was fine.

As we got to know our new cat, we learned something else very surprising about her. Early on she showed she had that strong personality with some high anxiety. But she was actually an obsessive-compulsive disorder (OCD) cat. At first we kind of joked about it, but we stopped joking about it once we realized that animals can be obsessive-compulsive just as much as humans can be. Sometimes Kit Kat was fun to watch in her OCD mess, but sometimes she was hard to watch. Either way, once our cat got something in her head, logical or not, she figured out how to achieve her preferred outcome unless she could be distracted from it.

Joe happened to have his own OCD ways. We used to joke with each other about it. But it made him in sync with Kit Kat in a way that evaded me. I first saw this one day when I walked into Joe's office in the Moscow house to ask him something.

"Wait," Joe said, interrupting me, "I almost forgot." He headed over to his two side-by-side wardrobes and opened the double doors of the one on the right. There on the very top shelf, sprawled across a row of Joe's shoes, lay Kit Kat. She was purring, and she was absolutely glassy-eyed.

"Umm . . . what's going on?" I said.

"She's 'cooking,'" Joe answered, as if that made perfect sense. "Time to move to the other closet," he sang. He lifted the languid and blissed-out Kit Kat, opened the other wardrobe, and laid her over its shoes on the top shelf. He shut the door. "She'll cook in there for a while now," Joe said. He returned to his desk.

I forgot why I'd come in. "Joe, what's going on?"

"Kit Kat likes to be shut inside my closets."

"Why?"

Joe looked at me like I was an idiot. "I guess because the closets smell like me."

"But how did you figure this out? I mean, specifically, how did you know she'd like to be shut in on a top shelf with the door closed?"

He shrugged. "I know her."

Of course the longer answer was that not only did Joe understand Kit Kat's temperament, he himself was as ritualistic as a cat. He would be the one to come up with solutions any time that kitty-OCD reared its head—like the situation we found ourselves in on laundry days.

We do laundry a little differently and always have. Except for linens in winter, we air-dry everything. In summer, we hang it all outside. In cold or wet weather, we air-dry clothes on large metal dryer racks in the living room.

Having been a bachelor for so long, Joe continued to do his own laundry once we married, which included hanging his clothes on the air-dryers. Kit Kat liked to watch Joe perform this activity. Once he was finished, she marched over and pulled everything down, including every single sock, which he would wash by the dozen. She was absolutely obsessed with pulling down Joe's wet laundry. Not mine; only Joe's. She literally sat down at the dryer, reared up with her claws extended, and yanked everything that was Joe's down into a wet pile. And she was fast.

What to do? First Joe put her in the bedroom with me while he hung laundry, but she simply waited at the threshold for him to open the door. Then she beelined for the air-dryer faster than that little round body should have been able to move and pulled a pile of laundry down with her claws, often using both front paws at the same time, before Joe could grab her.

Joe's next solution was to put her in the bathroom while he hung his laundry. When he opened the bathroom door, however, he made certain her food dish was within sight. Sure enough, she marched to the food dish and ate with gusto, laundry forgotten. Completely. Once she was satiated, Kit Kat didn't go back to the laundry and pull it down. She was over it.

"Why does that work?" I asked Joe.

"It breaks the loop in her mind," he responded.

"How did you know to do that?"

Again, he shrugged. "I know her."

This was not my first rodeo with an OCD pet.

When I was a child, our little wirehaired terrier Mugs gave birth to six puppies in the old stone smokehouse just beyond our kitchen door. Her baby-daddy was the beagle from the farm next door. Spaying and neutering were not the norm in rural Michigan in the fifties, and pet dogs were free-roaming. So babies were made.

This was exciting stuff for me to have these puppies, and it was especially welcome because it happened around the time my parents were going through their divorce, which, needless to say, was not a happy time. Because of the divorce, my mother was working at an outside job for the first time since having children. I was attending kindergarten, and my live-in grandmother greeted me at home when I returned from school midday. While that provided stability, it also reminded me why my mother was not there to greet me. Which then reminded me of everything else that was off.

Grandma used a wheelchair, which confined her to one area of the house. My sister was in school all day while I was there only half the day, so I didn't see much of her; plus it was already her nature to cope with the changes afoot by staying away from the house as much as possible. Neighbors with children were not close. I often found myself alone. I actually preferred to be at school.

But now that there were puppies, I could not wait to get off the school bus. I changed into play clothes and let Grandma know I was going outside. I would then hurry to the most wonderful thing.

Momma Mugs and her six puppies lived in the stone smokehouse, and it had a gothic-looking wooden door with an iron handle. When I lifted the noisy handle and opened that creaky door, noon light edged across the dirt floor. Then I could see all those little tails inside start to wag in tiny circles. I could hear the yipping and the snorting and the happy sounds puppies make.

Now I would turn around and quickly drop to the ground. I'd stretch straight out on my stomach and cover the sides of my face with my hands. The puppies would scamper outside and crawl all over me and lick whatever skin they could find. They'd sniff and yip and carry on and try to get to my face with their little wet noses. They'd chew on my long braids. They especially loved licking my ears. I giggled and giggled. I was a happy Gulliver in the Land of Lilliput, but no little creatures had to tie me down; I stayed on the ground willingly. It made me so happy I forgot my family troubles for a while every day. This was an event in my life I still mentally go to when I need calming today.

The puppies of course grew up. Five found homes, and

sadly, Mugs was killed by the school bus. We kept one puppy—an odd-looking little guy named Buster. He was born when I was in kindergarten, and he lived until the spring I graduated from high school, so he truly was the dog of my youth.

Buster was a solid, thick dog with skinny legs, about the size of a boxer. He had patches of black and white and beige all over his body and face. His body hair was coarse, bordering on his mother's nappy texture, but his head had straight hair and a terrier face. His eyebrow hairs covered parts of his dark eyes, and when he looked around, those hairs would move. His personality was sweet, and we all loved him.

Buster had the most endearing habit of sitting up on his haunches with his paws in the air. He would do this for anyone, stranger or kin—and he could hold the pose for the longest time, casting shy glances at the person from under those hairy eyebrows. It was sometimes a greeting, sometimes an appeal, sometimes a little show-offy because he knew humans would fawn over him. He was quite adorable.

But Buster was obsessive and phobic about many things. When he was frightened, first he would shake. Hearing Buster's dog tags rattle in terror is a strong memory for both my sister and me. He would slink along behind whatever human was around, close enough to trip the person. He did not want to be left alone. Although he was terrified of car rides, he would rather travel than be left alone. He'd hunch over on the floor of the car and shake and drool the entire way, be it five minutes or five hours. My mother started giving him a tranquilizer for the four-hour trip to our lake cabin in northern Michigan. I don't recall if it helped.

If Buster was left alone indoors for any length of time, he could be destructive, even as an adult. I recall once he was accidentally shut in my parents' bedroom, and while we were away, he chewed out the entire bottom of the door so he could get out.

He was terrified of storms—and equally terrified of the approach of storms. It could be a dry day with a clear blue sky, not a cloud in sight—but if at some point Buster started to shake and get clingy, you didn't plan your picnic. He was never wrong. Soon enough, we'd hear a distant rumble. Our dog was Doppler radar, long before television meteorologists began so casually using the term—long before they were even called meteorologists.

So the two most horrifying things in Buster's life were separation and bad weather. And if we were not home and the weather started changing for the worse, it was a double whammy. If Buster was outside, he ran. I've since learned that being an indiscriminate runner is a beagle thing, so I guess that confirms Buster's paternity.

If the weather was growing worrisome when my sister and I were at school, we would watch the sky outside those huge classroom windows, both of us getting a little sick to our stomachs, thinking the same thing in our different class-rooms: *Where's Buster?* If he became fearful while outdoors, he would run and run, and eventually my mother would get calls from strangers who stopped to pet the adorable dog sitting up in their driveway and read his dog tags.

But the year after my sister left home, Buster discovered my high school a quarter mile down the road and set back in a field. He learned that this brick building housed a lot of friendly people. I was there, too, but that didn't really matter—it only mattered that now he was no longer alone, and any nice human would do.

So on those warm spring days when Buster might sense a storm approaching and he was outside, he would first shake and scratch at our front door. If nobody answered, he would take off in a dead panic, running alongside the road from our house straight to the school. If the school doors were propped open, which they were on warm days, Buster was in luck. Once inside he roamed the halls, shaking and rattling his dog tags, until he saw a human, whereupon he would make his move: stop, sit up, and offer shy little glances from under his shaggy eyebrows.

My high school had a few hundred people in it, and it was not long before they all knew and loved Buster. Once when I saw him in the hall outside my classroom, my best friend also saw him and quietly called him in by name. He marched right up to the teacher herself and did his sitting up trick for her. She was immediately smitten. The day would come when I would hear over the intercom from the front office, "Lonnie, Buster's here . . ."—only that—and it was understood that unless I was taking a test, I was expected to walk my friendly, frightened, obsessive dog home and tuck him back indoors.

Not long ago, my sister and I admitted to each other that, to this day, even though neither of us is afraid of storms, we each get momentarily a little nervous when we hear thunder in the distance. We automatically think: *Where's Buster?*

Like my sweet dog from childhood, Kit Kat was worth the time we took to accommodate her issues. She would pay back that special attention with interest many times and for many years.

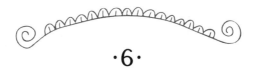

·6·

MY FEATHERED
FRIEND

To wonder at an animal is to begin to
understand God.

Unknown

Kit Kat would not be our only stray at the Moscow house.
We were presented with a temporary pet shortly after Kit
Kat moved in. And this one stayed outdoors.

The stray appeared on a lovely morning on the first of May.
Joe and I sat on the patio, which was a fine place to hang out
for a short period of time each year. We had a few weeks to
use the open patio before the mosquito—Michigan's "state
bird"—would make its appearance. As we enjoyed the balmy
morning air, we heard noises we didn't recognize coming
from under the yew bushes next to us—rustling noises from

some creature. Wild critters as a rule would be quieter, so what was this?

Joe peered under a bush. "It's a chicken," he announced.

I found this hard to believe. "Are you sure?"

"I'm sure."

While it was true that we lived in the country, I'd not seen any chickens in the immediate vicinity. Why would one be at our house?

"It's little and it's black," Joe said. He watched the chicken for a minute. "Should we feed it?"

"I'm not sure what chickens eat," I said, but I went indoors to rustle up something. I remembered they liked to pick things off the ground, but that was about it. I pulled together some unsalted peanuts and popcorn, shook it onto the ground, and the chicken did indeed come forth and eat.

Joe and I settled back into our patio chairs and watched the chicken eat its breakfast. When I was a kid, the neighbors next door had chickens, but I paid no attention to them back then. Knowing little to nothing about chickens, I assumed this was a rooster—maybe because we had had a stray rooster when I was a child. He had appeared from nowhere and crowed us awake each morning for a month or so before disappearing one day.

So now, partly because of this chicken's assertive nature and partly because of its extraordinarily beautiful comb, I figured that we had a rooster. The bird was small and compact, raven-black, and its deep red comb extended in red leathery seams into its face. We both agreed this little rooster was quite handsome. And hungry. And noisy. He picked at the snacks and clucked and waddled around us as we sat on the patio.

I figured the rooster had wandered off his farm somewhere, and I figured he'd return to his farm. In fact, I didn't expect him to be with us the next day, but there he was on the patio. He seemed to expect to be fed. We decided he could stay if that's what he wanted.

This time the appropriate name came to us quickly: Albert, after my beloved stepdad Al who had died a few months before and whose birthday was that very day. And because Dad absolutely would not eat poultry. In our house when I was growing up, we only had poultry on the dinner table on Thanksgiving and on my birthday.

I called my sister and brother-in-law to ask about proper food for chickens since they had a handsome flock of noisy, chattering guinea fowl roaming their property. My brother-in-law Dick showed up and supplied us with a big bag of chicken feed. And some news.

"That's not a rooster," Dick said. "That's a hen."

Joe and I looked at the chicken. "How do you know?" I asked.

Dick laughed. "How do I know? I know because I know. She's a banty hen."

So we changed Albert to Alberta. It seemed even more appropriate to name her Alberta because I remembered Dad saying that he bought his first Model T at age thirteen and paid for it with a box of banty hens.

Now we had a new daily chore with our new little pet. We went out the west patio door to feed Alberta in the morning, and she was always waiting. If we weren't out there early enough, she would leave the patio, march around to the front of the house, hop up on the porch, and make all kinds of racket at the front door. Clearly she and Kit Kat had been separated at birth in that regard. Since we never fed Alberta on the front porch, it was as if she somehow knew where we slept. We would laugh and invite her back to the patio for her meal. She laid little eggs all over the place—the best spot being the basement window wells.

And where was Kit Kat during all this? Our new hen's existence absolutely tortured our cat and her fine-tuned prey instincts. Alberta was a bird, after all. Kit Kat would usually not be a cat to rush an open door—living outdoors had clearly been stressful for her, and she knew she had a good gig indoors. But twice during the first month Alberta lived with us, Kit Kat shot out the patio door before I could stop her, and she lunged for Alberta.

Fortunately Alberta's wings were not clipped, and she was faster than Kit Kat. She simply sailed up to the high branches of a maple tree, which was too huge for good cat climbing. And Alberta would wait it out. Kit Kat would slink under the yews and watch for her next opportunity, which never happened because I would call for Joe to come get Kit Kat—he was faster than I, and I was panicked that my cat would run to the highway and be killed. Always that's where my mind went. I was so upset once that Joe reluctantly ran out in his underwear to retrieve Kit Kat from under the yews.

We became more vigilant about monitoring Kit Kat at Alberta's feeding time. But whenever I fed the chicken, I could see Kit Kat watching from the window with a primitive expression on her usually placid face. The expression clearly said "kill." I now fully understood how she made it back to us safely.

A few days after Alberta's arrival, I decided to do some planting around the outside of the house—begonias and geraniums, a few hostas. I bought soil, pots, and plants and started the work. But I soon stopped. In the past I had found balcony gardening in the city to be a good relaxer for me, but here and now, the tasks involved seemed overwhelming. Anxiety and depression seemed to be playing catch inside me that spring as we moved into summer, and at times it was taking over my day. As I stumbled through planting, I finally sat down on the patio and put my face in my hands.

Then I sensed a presence at my feet. I opened my eyes and there stood Alberta on the grass nearby. She had already eaten. She was standing near me apparently because she wanted to. So, as is my habit with living creatures in general, I started talking to her. She cocked her head and watched me. I was reminded of the one-sided conversations with my childhood cat Boots when it seemed like she understood me.

This turned into a daily thing for me, talking to Alberta. I was surprised to discover that I found it helpful to speak to this hen who seemed to like hanging around me, no matter what my mood. Studies exist that show the combination of talk therapy and physical exercise is as effective as antidepressants for some people. I doubt any of the studies examined talking to hens, but I do know it was helpful for me while puttering outside to talk to Alberta.

I hired a couple of college boys to help finish the initial planting. They were good guys, funny and full of youthful energy, and it turned into a pleasant day that lifted my spirits considerably. Of course, Alberta joined us in our work. She followed us around the yard. Maybe all hens are this sociable, but she seemed to think she was part of the gang. And the guys loved her. Every time they dug up a worm, they'd toss it to her, and she caught it mid-air. She snacked well that day. And by day's end, I had a garden where Alberta and I could hang out together. Indeed, every morning she'd join me while I fussed about.

My mother turned eighty that May, and we held a big family celebration at our place. The weather was good, mosquitoes still at bay, so we held the party on the patio. In preparation for company, Joe raked up our acre's worth of winter's leftover branches and blown leaves. This took him about three hours, during which Alberta followed him the entire time, sometimes perching on the yew bushes, sometimes bobbing contentedly nearby in the grass. This was Joe's first experience with her being his buddy in the yard, and I heard him talking to her too.

When the guests arrived and gathered on the patio, Alberta perched on the patio's edge and mingled. Everyone oohed and aahed over her pretty blue-black feathers and her sociable nature. She was a hit.

All summer Alberta stayed with us. We fed and watered her and discovered her eggs here and there. She was almost eating out of Joe's hand. I would often sit on the patio steps and watch her edge closer to me, yet keep a little distance. I cooed over her and prayed my gratitude that this little hen came along to distract me from my darkness.

Alberta also somehow helped me focus on my outdoor tasks. Was it just a matter of having living company? Or was it some connection we humans instinctively know about and act on but don't think about?

My friend Ed was a rookie teacher straight out of the Peace Corps in the late sixties. He took a job teaching third grade in inner-city Flint. A stray cat appeared at the school, and Ed got permission to keep the cat in the classroom. These were different times, of course, and amazingly the cat lived at the school. The kids named him Frisky.

Most of Ed's students had no experience with cats, so he was able to educate them on cats and allow them to experience Frisky on an individual level. Ed used Frisky to kick off any number of subjects—learning weights and measures by assessing Frisky, writing about what the kids thought Frisky might have done over the weekend, that sort of thing.

These were the days before Attention Deficit Hyperactivity Disorder (ADHD) in children was named. But Ed observed that the kids with the most concentration problems responded to Frisky in surprising ways. Petting a cat sprawled across a desk apparently better allowed a child to focus and do his or her schoolwork. Of course today there are a number of studies on such a phenomenon. I don't have ADHD. But depression and anxiety can cause new things to kick in for a while, like trouble focusing and concentrating. That was happening with me. I saw for myself that not only did the presence of Alberta in my yard soothe me emotionally but I was able to focus better on the tasks before me with her by my side.

In the years to come, I would see that with my cats as well. Midst a background of purring, I was going to become very productive.

Of course rural Michigan had any number of wild things that could hurt Alberta—the very reasons we had wanted Kit Kat to live somewhere with better shelter. But Alberta stayed safe at our house all summer, most likely because her wings were not clipped. She was a wonderful outdoor pet. But as we moved into September, we knew she could not survive without shelter. So we put the word out: Would someone like a pet hen? And, of course, not eat her?

Someone would. My niece and her family lived about fifteen miles away and were willing to take her to add to their growing menagerie. We knew it was necessary to let her go, though I hated to do it.

The day finally came when Joe and I sat on the patio with Alberta and told her where she was going and why. We put some feed in the bottom of a laundry basket on its side. She waddled around it, then walked in and began to nibble. We slowly righted the basket and put the lid on it, then drove to my niece's place.

Sure enough, there were pets galore there—dogs, cats, cows, a horse, a billy goat—and in particular, one fat, friendly hen named Goldilocks who would become Alberta's best friend. Goldilocks also had unclipped wings, and she too laid eggs wherever she wished. At night the two of them roosted in a shed, protected by the noisy billy goat.

Alberta was in a good place, and I wouldn't have to worry about her. I understood she had come to my house for only a season, and I could let her go.

Alberta was not the last beautiful creature to show up at our house and ask to stay. The next one would come to the back door the following year on a very cold day in November—and she would be covered in fur, not feathers.

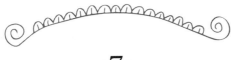

·7·

THE BLUE CAT

A meow massages the heart.

Stuart McMillan

It was early evening on the cusp of Thanksgiving week, an evening with a powerful wind. At such times in Michigan we note the windchill factor, and it was a scant thirteen degrees, unseasonably cold for November. No snow lay on the ground, but clearly winter was edging its way in.

I had finished running around doing errands that evening, and I had holidays on my mind as I drove home. This would be the second Thanksgiving for Joe and me in our old house, and this time we were looking forward to having guests. It would be my first time to host my family for a holiday.

In San Francisco, from my first year there, I hosted Thanksgiving in my one-bedroom apartment for people I knew who, like myself, had no family nearby. There would be anywhere from five to fifteen people, and I made sure it was a sit-down dinner, served on real china and linens, all of us seated at a long row of folding tables. A dear friend who loved to cook actually flew up from Los Angeles every year and prepared a traditional feast. We would spend the rest of the day stoking the fireplace, watching the fog roll by, and talking. When Joe and I married, we continued the tradition.

Now we could do all that with my family in our old house. It would be quieter, but it would be fine.

I was adjusting to this quieter life, thanks in large part to the company I had all day in Kit Kat. She was a tremendous companion, truly a writer's cat. Like most cats, she loved to hang around books and paper. With Kit Kat by my side, I had managed to write a couple of books for young readers and many published poems.

It was already dark when I pulled into our driveway. The shadowy tops of the seven maple trees around the house shook in the wind. I looked forward to getting inside and brewing up some decaf coffee. Then Kit Kat and I would curl up together and wait for Joe to come home from work. I would watch the news while Kit Kat watched for Joe.

I parked in the driveway, turned off the engine, and opened my car door. That's when I heard it. The wind came heartily from the southwest and blustered around the corner of the house, and it was an audible wind, strong enough to seem like a living thing. With it came the cry of a small animal.

I figured the cries would stay in the dark for a while, and maybe I'd eventually see a critter. But as soon as the utility light at the back door flashed on, out of the blackness sprang the most gorgeous kitten I had ever seen. Her coat was a solid blue-gray, and she was so beautiful and so panicked that I'm embarrassed to say I actually burst into tears.

The kitten beat me to the door and expressed tremendous relief at seeing me. Of course, intense rubbing and purring kicked in, those amazing ways of a feline in need. This kitten seemed to be a very different kind of stray than Kit Kat had been. Kit Kat had asked us for food from a distance and stayed away from humans other than Joe. The closest she had come to the house was only close enough to be seen from a window.

But it was clear that this little one had been around people enough to know to come to them for protection, and she was using everything in her power to get it. Once I understood this, my heart broke for her. I dropped my bags and bent down to pet her, trying to get a grip on my emotions.

I knew the kitten needed food and warmth, but I believed I could not bring her inside because of Kit Kat. But I could at least feed her outside. I gently pushed her away from me while I unlocked the back door, and I had quite a time keeping her from going in. I told her I'd be right back, but of course she didn't believe me. I nudged her away with the toe of my shoe and managed to get myself indoors, where I opened a can of cat food and filled a dish of water.

When I opened the back door again, I was surprised to see that the kitten had managed to tuck herself in between the storm door and the back door. There she huddled on the threshold, trying to get warm. I nudged her gently off the threshold and stepped back outside with her, talking in soothing tones. I placed the dishes on the deck, and she hunkered down to eat. Then I hurried back indoors while her back was turned and watched her from the window.

The problem was that Joe and I didn't believe we could have another pet with Kit Kat. Our girl was a tough little thing. Or rather, a tough big thing now—she'd gotten pretty hefty. I met a guy once who laughingly described his cat as one who carried a knife, and in some respects, we probably could have said the same about Kit Kat, even though all that toughness housed a truly soulful creature.

But Kit Kat had fended for herself outside too long to get along with competition. She was an absolute sweetheart unless confronted by another creature, and then that swamp cat personality was in full form. She backed my mother's dog right into a corner. We never considered bringing in another cat—we figured on her own territory, Kit Kat might kill the competition. Joe and I had discussed it early on and had come to the decision that our house would be Kit Kat's castle. We wanted her to have a long and happy life here with us, catching farmhouse mice, sleeping on sunny windowsills, biting our toes awake in the morning. It was enough.

Through the window, I saw Joe pull up from work. I had calmed down as I watched the kitten work her way through the can of food. Joe walked in the door and looked at me. "So what's the story out there?"

I didn't know what was wrong with me, but I started crying again. "It's a stray," I blubbered. "We can't leave it out there or it'll freeze to death. And we can't have it inside with Kit Kat. She'll kill it."

Joe nodded and thought for a minute. "We haven't put any furniture in that east bedroom upstairs since we painted it." It was true. We still didn't use the upstairs, which was shut off from the main floor with a door at the top of the stairs. The upstairs rooms were full of storage and extra furniture, except the one room that had been recently painted. "We have another litterbox," Joe said. "Let's put the kitten in the empty room until we can figure out what to do. At least it will be warm and safe and away from Kit Kat."

It was a good plan. "Okay," I sniffed. I put Kit Kat in the basement as Joe headed out the back door. When he brought in the kitten on its back, we confirmed it was a she, and her purr was so noisy it preceded her like an announcement. I've since learned that kittens have loud purrs so that Momma can hear them. Well, this momma definitely heard her.

"Careful," Joe said, "her nose is bleeding. She may be sick."

We wrapped her in my pink bath towel, and I held her on her back like a baby. The kitten purred and wiggled, and tears sprang up in me again. I felt like an idiot.

"I don't know if she's bleeding from her nose or if it's a scrape," Joe observed, looking her over. We figured she was around five months old, with a soft, thick coat the shade of gray that animal people call blue—one solid color from her triangular head to her tapered paws, even her straight nose and velvety ears. She gazed back and forth at us, purring, her green eyes peering out of that smoky coat like headlights in fog.

"Wow," said Joe. "This cat could be in a calendar." It was true. She was perfectly made. I started to calm down again once I realized her exceptional beauty would guarantee her a home with someone. In fact, it was hard to imagine anyone giving up this lovely creature with what already seemed to be a winning personality.

Eventually Joe took her from me. "I'll get her bedded down," he offered. "She's probably exhausted."

Never was there a happier feline than the blue kitten that night. We made her a bed in a box with an old sweater of mine to keep her warm, and Joe took her upstairs. I realized later that, between the towel and the sweater, she learned to take comfort from my scent right away. Joe fixed up a litterbox for her, and fortunately this little beast knew exactly what to do. She leaped right in and had a private moment. She devoured another bowl of food, purring the entire time, then curled up in her new bed and watched from under heavy eyelids as Joe puttered around her new room. Her relief at being able to safely rest with a full tummy was palpable.

Downstairs, I stayed on the phone, trying to find her a home. For a couple of hours I called everyone I knew, to no avail. I gave it my all. What a wonderful Christmas present she'd be for your kids, I told people, and we'd be happy to keep her until then. We'll take care of her shots and have her spayed. We'll even deliver her in her own carrying case! I felt like a car salesman throwing in extra options to make his quota at the end of the month. Except that this kitten really *was* a deal. Such a deal that I knew that once again Joe was going to have to be the one to tend to her needs so I could avoid getting attached to her.

The next morning, when Joe went upstairs to feed the kitten, he saw that she had cleaned herself up. Now it was clear that her nose was merely scraped. In a few days, we took her to our new vet for a checkup and vaccinations. She purred through the entire appointment—even the shots.

The kitten stayed upstairs in her room for the next several days. At first she kept rather quiet, and we figured she was getting rested up from her harrowing time outdoors. We guessed she'd not been outside long, but certainly she'd expended plenty of energy and adrenaline during that time trying to survive.

A few days later, Joe put Kit Kat in the basement and then brought the kitten downstairs, thinking I might want to hold her. He was oh so right. I had been avoiding her so that I would not get attached, but I was itching to touch that soft little creature. I placed her on her back and cradled her in my arms. She let me cuddle her, rub her belly, even gently separate each of her toes. She always kept her claws in. At one point she stretched out her front paw and placed it on my cheek, keeping it there while she gazed into my face.

Oh dear. How was I going to give her away?

For the next few weeks, the kitten lived in a room of her own. When Joe poured new litter into her box, she sat on his shoulder to watch. When he poured dry food into her dish, she dove under the bag and let the food pellets rain on her. When he rolled the trash can to the roadside in the moonlight or raked leaves in the front yard in daylight, she watched from a tall upstairs window. She pounced on any toy we gave her, especially rubber balls—she played and played with them in her otherwise empty room.

As for me, I would lie in bed in the room below early in the morning and late at night and listen to the kitten roll the ball back and forth on the pine floor planks, then scamper after it. Though technically I refused to name a cat we were giving away, in my heart I named her. All that rolling of the ball made me think of the late, great comedienne Lucille Ball. In my heart, I named the kitten Lucy.

We had our Thanksgiving dinner with a long table of relatives at our place. It was a very nice day. Joe was amazed by the worker-bee women of my family—by the time everyone left, the leftovers had been turned into soup and stew and tucked into the freezer.

The following day, we began decorating the house for Christmas. We picked out a tall, pungent Fraser fir that would allow just enough room for an angel to perch atop it without brushing the twelve-foot-high ceiling of the dining room. We brought the tree home and let it stand a few days undecorated so Kit Kat could sniff at it and adjust to it. That had worked well the year before during her first Christmas indoors.

Then I began pulling out the ornaments. Kit Kat settled down on the back of the couch and tucked in her front paws. She inhaled the new scents in the room—the tree, the spicy scented candles—and watched the blinking Christmas lights. My family, as indulgent with their pets as we were with ours, had sent wrapped gifts for Kit Kat, which we placed under the tree. Of course, family members would receive back from Kit Kat—what else?—Kit Kat candy bars.

At the back of my mind nagged the future prospects of The Little One, as we were calling the kitten. I continued to try to find her a good home. Over the next few weeks, three different families each gave a definite yes. Then at the last minute, for a variety of reasons, none could take her. This was frustrating, because I knew that if anyone would hold her just once, they'd walk away with her. I knew this because I'd fallen in love with her myself.

I gave in and began going upstairs every day, several times per day, to give the kitten attention. She was getting pretty lonely and bored up there by herself, almost panicky when we'd leave her. So every day I played with her, then placed her on her back and held her in my arms. She would literally gaze up at me and heave a sigh, the picture of contentment while I rocked her.

I knew from holding Kit Kat that cats like to be rocked; we all came from the waters of the womb. So I'd rock the kitten, rubbing her chest and belly. I'd heard from some cat rescuers that it's good to get kittens adjusted to being touched on their bellies and all over their bodies. The kitten allowed me to do this, and she'd reach her paw up to my face, sometimes both her paws, to press against my chin, purring and looking into my face. Sometimes she'd chew on my hair. To say I was smitten would be an understatement. But I refused to speak her secret name out loud. I redoubled my efforts to find her a good home before it became too hard to let her go.

I am a praying person. I pray about many things, but with so much misery in the world, should I beseech God on behalf of one blue kitten in winter? I decided, yes, the creatures of the world are here for reasons beyond my understanding. So as I rocked the kitten, I prayed for her future.

But after so many close calls for a home for her, I began to feel a little panicky. Who else could I call? And one day after she'd been with us just over a month, I heard inside, *She's yours.*

I protested right back inside. "I can't have her. We have Kit Kat."

Again I heard, *She's yours.*

This was a voice that had never failed me before. It was the same voice that in the past had kept me out of danger. The same voice that told me to up and move clear across the country by myself from New York to a job in San Francisco when I could hardly bear to do it, a voice that clearly said, *I have something there for you.*

In San Francisco three years later, the time came when I sensed I was going to lose my job. On the very day that I was laid off, that voice inside me warned me while I was at my desk that *this* would be the day. And after my boss let me go at 3:00 that afternoon, I walked outside, looked at the sky, and spoke out loud: "You said you had something here for me." And the voice said, *It wasn't the job.*

The following year, I met Joe right around the corner from my apartment. We married five months later, never doubting that we belonged together.

I do understand that one should be careful when one says an inside voice speaks to them. I have a good friend who is prone to psychotic breaks. She also has a good sense of humor, and when I've told her about hearing this voice at rare times, she laughs and says, "We have medication for that."

But as I've said, I'm a praying person, and I believed I was being nudged with words to tell me I was keeping this kitten. I quieted down and let the idea settle in. I rocked the kitten a bit more, then put her in her box-bed and went downstairs.

I called Joe at work, and without my bringing any of this up, he said, "You know, some people here at the office are sure we can get the cats together if we take our time with them. Apparently there are ways to do it. So I was thinking, let's keep The Little One. We'll both be home the week between Christmas and New Year, and we can use that time to get her together with Kit Kat."

I was stunned that Joe and I would be so in sync about this. And I realized it made perfect sense. We certainly could use our time off to get the cats together. Maybe it could work. Maybe the kitten really was ours.

I went back upstairs, picked the kitten up, and for the first time whispered into her satiny ear, "Lucy . . ."

She purred and purred.

·8·

DONNA THE PET
EXPERT

If cats could talk, they wouldn't.

Nan Porter

Kit Kat, of course, being a very smart cat, knew we had another creature living upstairs. At the whiff of the kitten on Joe's shirt that first blustery night, our expressive Kit Kat hissed and pushed right off Joe's chest with her hind legs like a rabbit. So for a few days, we actually changed our shirts and washed our hands after we visited upstairs. After all, we initially didn't intend to keep the kitten, so why upset our Kit Kat?

Lest we seem overindulgent—and then some—let's remember that Joe and I were very green to the indoor cat world. Kit Kat, once she made friends with the litterbox, had managed her adjustment to the house without much help from us—maybe even in spite of us. When I look back on it, it's clear to me that we did a whole lot wrong.

At any rate, when the blue kitten moved in upstairs, Joe and I changed our shirts after visiting her so as not to upset Kit Kat. That was foolish. We should have been letting both beasts smell the other however we could without having them meet face-to-face. We noticed over the days that Kit Kat's initial revulsion to the kitten's odor changed to curiosity. So we stopped changing our shirts. Kit Kat sniffed our clothes and hands at great length and with much interest when we came downstairs from visiting the new arrival.

Eventually Kit Kat began sitting on the bottom step of the staircase, watching us climb the stairs, then waiting for us to return from dealing with the kitten. There was a closed door at the top of the stairs, and though Kit Kat never ventured up there, she watched us traipse up and down the steep steps, her expression calm but curious.

On the first day of our Christmas vacations, Joe and I decided we had put off long enough a face-to-face introduction of Kit Kat and the newly named Lucy. It was time to give it a try. So one night, as the lights twinkled on the tree, Joe brought Lucy downstairs. Her little face swiveled around at the sights, that pretty blue nose twitching in the presence of new smells.

Kit Kat heard the now-familiar sound of the upstairs door squeaking open. She sashayed into the hall to investigate. At first she didn't notice anything unusual. But when Joe squatted down on the hallway floor, holding Lucy close to his chest, Kit Kat spied Lucy. Or maybe she smelled her. Or maybe she heard that mighty purr. At any rate, she locked eyes with Lucy, and the look on Kit Kat's face made both Joe and me uncomfortable. We both read it as: "Kill."

Kit Kat slowly approached the kitten and hissed. Then Kit Kat growled a long throaty growl. She hissed again. Then she growled again.

Lucy braced her front paws on Joe's arm but otherwise stayed still. She looked Kit Kat warily in the eye and leaned back against Joe's chest. Two things disturbed me. One was that Lucy actually scowled. I don't know how else to describe it. She raised her chin, lowered her upper eyelids, and scowled at Kit Kat. The other thing—and Joe noticed it, too—was that, for the first time since we'd known Lucy, she stopped purring.

Kit Kat carried on with the growling and the hissing. She slowly leaned forward and touched her nose to Lucy's, then drew back as if she'd been burned. And she hissed again. Joe and I looked at each other. This wasn't going well.

Now Kit Kat stomped down the hall and through the kitchen, headed for the basement door. I followed her. It was obvious that her adrenaline was pumping, and in my mind's eye, I saw a boxer punching at the air with aggressive energy. She stood at the basement door and waited for me to open it, her tail jerking around like crazy. Her eyes were bright and looked kind of scary.

"No, Kit Kat," I protested, "you don't want to go downstairs." Actually *I* didn't want her to go downstairs—I wanted her to be okay about everything. I leaned down to pick her up, and she hissed and tried to bite me. When I didn't open the basement door, she marched back to the bedroom and under the bed—her hiding place from the loud noises of thunderstorms, lawn mowers, vacuum sweepers, and the coffee-bean grinder—and now from interloping kittens. She didn't come out for a long time.

Joe returned Lucy to her room and came back downstairs rather solemnly. Everyone was upset after this showdown—both of the cats and both of us. In fact, I felt sick about it. We sat in the kitchen in silence. Finally I said, "This isn't going to work, is it?"

Joe shrugged. We sat for a moment until he spoke. "What about that pet expert you know? Do you think she could help?"

A member of a writing group I belonged to was a professional animal behaviorist. The daughter of a veterinarian and herself a licensed veterinary technician for many years, Donna now trained dogs and also offered her services to come into a client's home to assess and hopefully solve their unique pet problems. Or owner problems, as was often the case.

I knew that Donna had successfully helped one member of our writers group with her two house cats. One cat had intimidated the other cat into never leaving a bedroom. Donna observed them, then prescribed that the family should simply move their living room furniture around to a configuration that would no longer allow the dominant cat an all-points-view of the entire house. Apparently it had been able to glare down the other cat from a high perch and thereby exert territorial control. When the family moved the furniture around, the timid cat finally ventured out of the bedroom, and things improved from that day on. Who would have thought?

That was one of the less dramatic results Donna had with her work. She often regaled us at the writing group with stories about her clients—both the furry ones and their owners.

While Donna did not give an outward appearance of being a warm-fuzzy kind of animal lover, she actually had a deep love and respect for them. She understood animals in a way that seemed innate, though she explained it was simply because she had closely studied their behavior so as not to be injured in the examination room.

I had called Donna when Lucy first came to us, and she had approved everything we were doing—isolating the kitten, getting her spayed, and so forth. Donna was always so generous with free advice that it would be good to pay her for once.

I headed for the phone.

The day Donna came for her consultation, sparkling fields of snow around our house brightened the long farmhouse windows. I was relieved she was available and willing to drive to our remote location. She had suggested noon, and she arrived right on time.

I brewed a pot of coffee, and Donna, Joe, and I sat down at the kitchen table. We caught up on news and shot the breeze for a while, dragging our feet, I suppose. After all, who really wants to initiate a conflict in their own home, even if it is with cats? Or maybe especially with cats.

Eventually Donna got us on track. "So tell me how it was when you got them together."

We gave her a full report. Joe added, "We're afraid Kit Kat will kill the kitten."

"That's not likely," Donna assured us. "Dogs kill dogs. Dogs kill cats. But cats rarely kill other cats. They don't have to kill each other because they rely on body language." She drained her coffee. "Come on. Let's go see the girls."

We found Kit Kat in our bedroom, curled on top of the bed. She raised her head when we came in and looked Donna in the eye with mild curiosity.

"Ah, a tortoiseshell," Donna said. "Is she kind of crabby?"

Well, yes . . . that was a good description. Maybe a bit understated.

"Tortoiseshells and calicos—three-colored cats—usually are," she said. She waved her hand in the air over Kit Kat while she talked. Kit Kat slowly reached up a front leg and extended her paw toward Donna, toes splayed, claws out, as if to respond to what had just been said about her.

Donna laughed and withdrew her arm. "Sorry, Kit Kat." She looked around. "Where's the other one?"

Joe climbed the stairs and fetched Lucy while Donna and I waited in the hall. Joe let Lucy walk down the stairs herself, always a sight. The house had been built in 1842, and the stairs were original and steep, each step measuring nine inches high, taller than Lucy herself. She took the steps one at a time, front paws down first, then back paws, in careful little bunny hops.

Donna stood at the newel post and watched Lucy's descent. "Ah, a Russian Blue," she said. At the time, I knew nothing about types of cats. I just thought she was a smoky-blue cat with unusual fur. "That's a good-natured breed," Donna said. "And she's a beauty."

Lucy reached the bottom step, her face taking in all the excitement. Our bedroom sat off the center hallway, and the stairs stood right outside the bedroom. Kit Kat hopped off the bed and strolled into the hall to investigate.

"Let's see what they do," Donna said.

Kit Kat spied the kitten and froze. Then she started to

slink in Lucy's direction. It was, as Yogi Berra said, déjà vu all over again, only this time Lucy was on her feet, not in Joe's arms. Lucy saw Kit Kat and stood still. We stepped aside as Kit Kat slowly approached Lucy, stopping and starting several times, hissing and growling long and loud. It was making me concerned.

"That hiss is involuntary," Donna remarked.

"It is?" I said. "Isn't it a threat?"

Donna shook her head. "Cats hiss when they're scared."

"Kit Kat's *scared*? Of what?"

"She's scared of a strange cat."

This had never occurred to me. "But Kit Kat's so much bigger than Lucy," I said. Lucy was only five pounds compared to Kit Kat's fifteen.

Donna shrugged. "Kit Kat doesn't know that."

Now that Lucy was on her own feet, she decided she might as well investigate this huge and amazing space outside her tiny world, in spite of Kit Kat's expressions of displeasure. So Lucy turned away from Kit Kat and bounded into the living room, which fed into the dining room. Kit Kat stayed in the hall and continued to growl, a really sickening sound to me. "It hurts to hear that," I finally admitted.

Donna shifted position and continued to watch the cats. "Hear what?" She glanced at me. "The growl?"

I nodded and watched as Kit Kat crouched and peeked around the living room doorway after Lucy.

"Her growling bothers you?" Donna laughed. "Listen . . . Let me tell you how Kit Kat's thinking. She's thinking: *I hate that cat. Where's that cat? I HATE that cat! Where IS that cat?* She's half irritated and half fascinated. Watch her—she's dying to interact."

None of this had occurred to me, but now that Donna had pointed it out, I could see immediately that it was true. While it wasn't the way I'd choose to interact with a new creature in my world—hissing, growling, slinking behind it—I could see that it was Kit Kat's way. I remembered then how she had reacted to Lucy's scent on us—upset at first, then curiosity. She clearly was curious, and yes, she clearly was nervous. I thought I knew my cat, but I'd been reading her all wrong.

Kit Kat scooted into the living room so she could keep her eye on Lucy. "Let's watch what they do," Donna said. We humans followed the felines at a distance until Lucy had circled the main part of the house, through the living room, the dining room, the end of the kitchen, back into the hallway. This took some time, as she not only had short kitten legs but she was totally enthralled with all that was in this new territory. Kit Kat crept along behind her, crouched low, looking to me like she was going to pounce on Lucy. But she never did.

They stopped full circle back at the newel post. We had been tiptoeing behind them like the Marx brothers in a movie, and at this point none of us could see Lucy, who had parked herself at the bottom of the stairs. But we could see Kit Kat, still growling, still hissing, still looking ferocious—and crouched behind the newel post, watching Lucy from around it.

"Check it out," Donna said. "Kit Kat is posturing, but look how she keeps a barrier between them. She stays on this side of the newel post and acts tough. I'll see what's going on from the other side."

Donna softly hotfooted back through the dining and living rooms and into the hall from the other doorway. Then she hooted. "Come here!"

95

We hurried after her to find Lucy at the foot of the stairs, rolling around on her back, baring her belly, peering at Kit Kat, batting benignly at air.

Donna laughed. "Look at Lucy. She's fearless. I'll admit I was a little worried about these two, but not now. This kitten is no fighter. She wants to play. She absolutely wants to engage Kit Kat. And that's good news."

Now Kit Kat's adrenaline caught up to her like it did a few days before. She spun around and marched into the bedroom.

"Where's she going?" Donna asked.

"Under the bed," I said. "She goes there when she's scared or wants to be left alone. When we first brought Lucy downstairs, Kit Kat wanted to go to the basement, but I didn't let her, so she went under the bed."

"Why didn't you let her in the basement?"

"I was hoping she could deal with things up here, I guess." Once I said it out loud, it sounded pretty idiotic.

Donna obviously thought so too. She looked at me like I was bright purple. "She basically *told* you what she wanted," she said. "She couldn't have told you any clearer if she'd spoken words. If she wants to be left alone, let her hide so she can calm down." Donna put her hands on her hips and heaved an exasperated sigh. "Why don't people listen to their pets when they're trying to communicate something? Close the bedroom door and let Kit Kat have some private time. We'll let this one"—she waved at Lucy, who had begun scampering around—"run laps and work off some of this energy."

So while Kit Kat took a time-out behind closed doors, Lucy ran laps around the house—literally. Along the way, she discovered a new world—another cat box, more food and water dishes, a real live tree with lights and hanging things that could be *batted*. And there were baseboard radiators, electrical cords—oh yeah, we had to watch her as if she were a toddler. We let her run—and she ran nonstop around that circle of rooms—until that little body was all worn out. She slowed down, and her eyes got droopy, but she would not curl up and sleep. Everything was way too thrilling.

As we followed Lucy around the house, Donna instructed us on how to take a few minutes at a time, a few times a day, to get the cats together, much like we just had, increasing the amount of time as we saw fit. Lucy could stay upstairs at night for as long as necessary until we felt the two could coexist overnight without our supervision.

"How long will it take for them to get along?" Joe asked.

"Can't really say," Donna replied. "And they may never get along as well as you want them to. Remember they will have a tussle or two, because house cats do that. Like, they may show up together at the food dishes and then sit back and box at each other. It doesn't mean anything. It's just one cat saying, 'You know the other day when you barged in here in front of me and ate first? Well, it ticked me off,' and then the other cat says, 'Oh yeah? Well, you annoy me all the time.' Then they bat at each other for a while and walk away and they're over it." She shrugged. "It's nothing."

She went on. "Make sure you have one more litterbox than you have cats so that neither of them can commandeer a box. When house cats act out, it's all about the cat box. And that's one thing you have some control over."

Joe fished Lucy out from behind the refrigerator. "Guess I better put a barrier there," he said.

Donna nodded. "Kitten-proof this house, and don't let

Lucy in the basement until she's bigger. Old unfinished basements like yours aren't safe for kittens. But let Kit Kat down there whenever she wants. She'll need some peace and quiet from this hyper little thing." She thought for a moment. "I wish one of these cats were a neutered male—two females can be pretty territorial. But based on what I saw today, I think you'll be okay."

She went on to tell us some of her animal success stories that relaxed us and made us laugh. By the time she packed up to go home, Joe and I were feeling like maybe things were going to work out after all. Donna left us with this: "When your cats sleep together in the same room, they're showing they trust each other. If they sleep together on the same piece of furniture, your problems are over."

I filed that away with the wish that one day both cats would sleep on the bed with us. Today, that wish seemed too huge to happen.

After Donna left, Joe scooped up a weary Lucy and took her upstairs to her room. She slept like the dead that night. I know how well she slept because I never heard a ball roll on the floor up there until late the next morning.

·9·

THE RESULTS

God made the cat to give humankind the
pleasure of caressing the tiger.

Victor Hugo

Starting the day after Donna's visit and for the following
week, Joe and I put the two cats together several times per
day. These were short sessions for the most part, and we took
our cues from Kit Kat. She started out with her usual hissing and growling, but she also made her intense interest in
Lucy crystal clear. Kit Kat never hurt Lucy or even tried to,
but when she'd had enough of the little kitten, Kit Kat let us
know by stomping into hiding or asking—er, demanding—to
be let into the basement.

As for Lucy, she also made clear what she wanted in her
more playful style. She wanted very much to interact with

Kit Kat. She expressed this not only by staring at Kit Kat and following her around but also by grabbing Kit Kat's twitching tail. Lucy seemed unable to stop herself. She even grabbed Kit Kat's tail while Kit Kat ate, truly a flirt with danger, since Kit Kat took food very seriously. But Kit Kat only snapped around, hissed at Lucy, and went back to her meal.

At the same time, Lucy seemed never to run out of ways to get into trouble. I could see how curiosity had indeed killed the proverbial cat. And this one was a handful and a half. We fished her out from behind bookcases and out of drawers, and once she got herself stuck in our living room's lobster-trap-turned-coffee-table. Joe made an adjustment to the netting so that wouldn't happen again. Her romping turned power strips off and remote-controlled televisions on, and once she chewed through a phone cord while I was talking to a client in California. That was the end of that conversation.

Joe and I believed that Kit Kat never seemed to catch on that we were responsible for bringing Lucy into the house. We wondered if Kit Kat figured this irritating little beast was as pesky to us as she was to her and that we were all in this predicament together. She never seemed upset with *us* when Lucy was around—only with Lucy. Sometimes she'd give us an exasperated look as if to say, "Can you believe this?"

This put to rest a silly fear of ours—that Kit Kat would change toward us. She did not. As soon as Lucy went back upstairs, Kit Kat mellowed out and was just as cuddly with us as she had always been.

Several times a day that holiday week, one of us tromped upstairs to get Lucy. Then she made her little bunny hops down the steep steps, her journey slowed because she couldn't stop looking around along the way. During these downstairs sessions, she sometimes ignored Kit Kat in favor of things like flashing lights on the Christmas tree, but more often she happily followed Kit Kat around the house. This decidedly unnerved Kit Kat, who preferred to keep some physical object between them.

One evening after an especially lengthy getting-to-know-you day, Lucy spied me reading on the bed. She got herself on top of our bed by clawing her way up the bedspread. She curled up next to me, purring, working hard to stay awake. Soon enough Kit Kat hopped on the bed too. Lucy's eyes grew round and alert, and though she stayed put, she watched Kit Kat's every move as if she were the most fascinating thing Lucy had ever seen. When Kit Kat eventually spied Lucy, it decidedly agitated her, and again came the hisses and the growls.

But Kit Kat stayed on the bed. She parked herself on one side of me and left Lucy alone on the other side of me. I was finally starting to understand. Kit Kat needed a barrier between her and another creature, and I was the barrier. I was a happy barrier, too, because I had both cats on the bed with me. That was good enough for now.

For New Year's Eve that year, Joe and I were invited to a party, our first since we'd moved to the hinterlands. I've always loved the beginning of a new year, and I liked to celebrate it with others. After Joe and I married, we hosted New Year's Eve gatherings in our North Beach apartment, and they were great fun.

Neighbors never complained about our North Beach parties. First of all, they were all invited. In this particular part of

San Francisco, New Year's Eve was celebrated loudly. There were police barriers up all over the neighborhood because it was a frisky one on New Year's Eve. We were not far from the midnight ball drop down the Transamerica Pyramid. So for our parties, guests either walked to us or took cabs because the crowds outside would mean no parking. Once I counted forty-five guests crammed into our one-bedroom apartment and spilled out onto the balcony—and even onto the roof.

Because quite a few writers, artists, and musicians attended, these guests had an almost childlike pleasure in being together. There was no "What do you do for a living?" kind of talk. One night I heard someone yelling into the telephone in the hall, "You have to come! Anybody who is anybody in North Beach is here! Anyone who's not a *lawyer* is here!" I'm not sure our guest list was that amazing, but we certainly enjoyed one another. Joe kept the music hopping, and guests danced. One time, Joe hauled out all our pasta pans and wooden spoons and led guests in drumming. The pasta pan lids never really fit the pans again.

Understandably, it was a huge letdown when we moved to rural Michigan in this regard too. First of all, we moved into our temporary housing on New Year's Eve itself that year. Exhausted, we fell into bed at 10:00. "We'll celebrate next year," Joe promised.

The next year we were coming down from an exhausting couple of months that included moving into the farmhouse. Long before the New Year hit at midnight, we were in deep sleep in the house on the quiet plain. We had skipped Christmas decorations that year too. We were simply too tired to unpack them. "We'll celebrate next year," Joe promised again.

But the next year was the paranoid one—the coming of the Big Deal Year of 2000. We had a lovely tree for the first time in our house. But a New Year's gathering was not an option. Nobody we knew even seemed willing to leave their houses, other than to make a last-minute run to stock up on batteries. There was no way they were driving out to Moscow. We fell into bed early that night too. At some point in the wee hours of 2000, I woke up to see if we still had electricity. We did. I went back to sleep.

Now, for the first time in years, we were going to dress up and go out on New Year's Eve. I was excited. We put Lucy and Kit Kat together for a couple hours one last time that night—or the last time that year, one could say. Then we parked Lucy in her upstairs boudoir before we headed out for the evening.

Downtown Jackson, Michigan, was full of people bundled up for what was called Eve on the Ave. Families came down for hot chocolate and music and the midnight dropping of a ball down City Hall, one of the tallest buildings in town. The gathering we attended was at the big flat of some friends of ours. They had bought an old brick commercial building from the Victorian era right smack dab in the middle of town, and they had fixed up the entire top floor as their home.

Joe and I spied some out-of-town friends we didn't get to see very often, and we all parked on couches and talked. Paul and Karen were foster care providers for their local Humane Society. They were very interested in the story of Lucy, and they brimmed with encouragement. They had heard of our animal behaviorist, Donna, and they approved of all we were doing to get the two cats used to each other. I admitted to them that things were better than they had been a week ago, but I still wondered if it would ever really be okay between Kit Kat and Lucy. They assured us it would be fine, that we only needed to give it time.

"Remember how our cat Muffin acted when we first got the dog?" Karen said to Paul. She turned to us. "Muffin would vomit on the dining room table every time she saw him." Paul nodded, and they both laughed heartily.

Joe and I glanced at each other in horror. We had a fresh appreciation for our well-behaved Kit Kat.

We arrived home at about 2:00 a.m. to find Kit Kat sitting in the kitchen window waiting for us. She always watched the driveway from this window if we'd been gone awhile. Once she saw the car pull in and park, she would make for the back door. We had two doors to unlock to get inside, and while unlocking the second door, Kit Kat could always be heard crying on the other side. Tonight she seemed especially distressed; we were usually all tucked into bed long before this.

In my opinion it's a myth that cats do not need company. Every cat I've ever had was totally thrilled to be in my presence— or in the presence of any member of the household—even if it had a uniquely feline way of showing it.

I have had cats cry when I left them and cry when I returned. When I was in high school, my family had a wonderful twenty-pound ginger male who would follow me to my car when I was about to leave. Then he would stand on his hind legs and place his paws on the car window and meow. Try to drive away from a cat like that.

Nevertheless, Donna claimed that female cats don't mind being alone and that we shouldn't worry about Kit Kat. "Even if they're spayed," she said, "females are hardwired to drive other cats out of their territory. They want to be alone."

Hardwired or not, Kit Kat didn't seem to like to be alone too much of the time. True, cats sleep two-thirds of their life, and so did Kit Kat. But during that waking third, she wanted company. Now in these wee hours of New Year's Day, Kit Kat let us know how glad she was that we were home. A mere few hours later, after refusing to let us sleep in, she rubbed on and hung around with us. Then we brought Lucy downstairs.

By now, Kit Kat expressed only irritation when she saw Lucy. We kept the girls together for six hours that day—the longest block of time so far—and they got along fairly well. Once again, they lay on the bed with me while I read, one on either side of me. This time Kit Kat actually fell asleep. I remembered Donna had said that whenever cats sleep in the same room, there's trust. To me, it seemed like a perfect way to start a new year.

Eventually Lucy fell asleep, too, something she never had done downstairs because of all the stimulation. When it was time for *me* to go to sleep, I carried Lucy upstairs and watched her drag her weary little self into her box-bed, curl into a ball, and close her eyes. All that togetherness wore her clean out.

Joe and I had a couple days before going back to work, and on one of those days, we had a family gathering to attend. The cats had been doing so well that we decided to leave them downstairs together while we were gone. They'd not yet spent the night—or any other time—together without us. But we felt this would be a good time for them to work things out.

By now I felt certain that Kit Kat would not harm Lucy, but

I still was afraid Lucy would get into some danger because of her amazing ability to get caught in places and have to be rescued. But we had cat-proofed the place as much as we could. She was six or seven months old now and was going to have to live without constant supervision. Besides, we wouldn't be gone long.

We came home after about four hours. Nobody was in the kitchen window waiting for us. That was unsettling. We unlocked the outside door, then the inside door. No Kit Kat crying for us.

Joe walked in ahead of me and stopped at the back of an easy chair in my mudroom office. As I wriggled out of my coat, he spoke to me quietly. "Come here."

I joined Joe and looked over the top of the chair. There on the seat was Kit Kat. She was spooned around Lucy, who was curled into a furry ball with her eyes squeezed shut. And Kit Kat was grooming her. Tenderly. No wonder there was no greeting at the door.

Joe and I grabbed hands and grinned stupidly at one another. Kit Kat stopped her task and looked up at us. She had the most gentle expression on her face.

One always runs the risk of anthropomorphizing when trying to figure out what's going on in the mind of an animal, even one you know well. But it seemed to both Joe and me that Kit Kat was thanking us for this little creature of her own species to share those many hours of being alone.

Kit Kat held our eyes a moment. Then she turned back to her work of grooming Lucy.

·10·

LUCY

When I play with my cat, how do I know
she is not actually playing with me?

Michel Eyquem de Montaigne

After we came home to find Kit Kat grooming Lucy, our kitten became a permanent member of the downstairs, never again to go upstairs. The first night she stayed in the bedroom with us, she seemed uncertain, probably thinking she was going back upstairs at some point. She watched us prepare for sleep from atop the bed. Once the lights were out, she fell asleep where she lay. In the morning I found her curled into a little ball on the corner of our big bed.

I had my wish. My cats had both slept with us. Now it was time for us to get to know Lucy better and see if she was more than a pretty face.

One of the many delightful things I discovered about our new kitten was that she smelled faintly like chocolate. Kit Kat smelled like a plush toy, but when I buried my nose in Lucy's fur, it smelled like chocolate. I never mentioned it to Joe. Then one day I heard Joe in the next room cooing over Lucy and saying, "How come you smell like cocoa? Huh? How come?"

Pet expert Donna had noted that Lucy was a Russian Blue when she met her. A word about that: There are breeders of Russian Blue cats all over the world, and I have met some of them over the years. I understand that simply because an animal looks like a particular breed doesn't necessarily make it so. For the purposes of this tale, I will refer to Lucy as Russian Blue. As a nod to professional breeders, however, I do understand that she's most likely Russian Blue-*ish*.

After our new blue kitten had been with us for a while, I started reading up on Russian Blues. Real Russian Blue or not, I discovered Lucy was true to the breed in every way. Dark blue double coat with silver tips all over her body. Triangular face with vivid green eyes. A perpetual smile when in profile. Calm and gentle personality. They seem to walk on their toes like ballet dancers. They dislike loud noises.

The gentle Russian Blue personality was one that Lucy would grow into, though, because as a kitten, she was just rambunctious. But she was sweet from the get-go. I will admit that compared to Kit Kat's strong personality, it was nice to have this gentler disposition in the house. Joe and I loved Kit Kat fiercely. But we also fell in love with this blue kitten in a different way, I suppose much like people who adore their firstborn child also fall in love with a new smiling baby.

My mother was already in Florida for the winter when

Lucy moved in with us. When I told Mom about Lucy's easy personality, she said in an excited voice, "Do you think she would let you put a doll's dress on her?"

Of all the things she could have said, I would never have thought of this. You can know your parents all your life, and they can still surprise you.

Could I put a doll dress on little Lucy? It seemed that this was my mother's measure of a wonderful pet, based on playing with barn kittens when she was a child. My measure of the ultimate pet from childhood was having a cat who would let me carry her around on my shoulder and would sleep on the bed with me. I had that with Kit Kat now, unless she was kitty-PMS-ing. But Lucy was more baby-like and, yes, more doll-like, though I never did try putting a dress on her.

Living as she had in her upstairs room, Lucy missed most of her first Christmas, but not all of it. We didn't take down our tree until around the fifth of January, and this item with its twinkling lights and hanging baubles was a source of much delight to Lucy. She was thrilled with more than one lower-branch ornament. We didn't use tinsel or any other object that she or Kit Kat could ingest, so they were pretty safe. Lucy did manage to pull down ornaments, which she batted around like a soccer player, and sometimes I'd see her trot out of the room with a soft ornament hanging from her mouth as if it were prey. For several months after Christmas, I found ornaments that had been batted under heavy furniture all over the house.

While I packed up the decorations after Lucy's first Christmas, she sat high atop the stacked plastic red and green storage bins, focused on my every action. Now and then I wadded used wrapping paper into a ball and tossed it her way. This was always appreciated. Kit Kat had been playful when she moved in, but only briefly, and it always seemed to involve claws. By now she was more blasé about moving objects that weren't living creatures. Lucy, however, played for all she was worth, leaping from any height to chase anything that moved, including wadded-up paper.

Even short-haired Russian Blues have a double coat of thick fur. Russian monks crossbred and raised the Blues for their fur. One of the myths of Russia is that soldiers draped the Blues over their shoulders to ride into battle with them. I've always felt this myth was a way to lie about why monks were breeding these cats in the first place—to wear their fur.

When Lucy's belly was shaved for her spaying, the fur didn't grow back for quite a while. Our vet explained that it would come in with a later cycle of hair growth. In the meantime, for several months, her belly was pink with a layer of peach fuzz. It reminded Joe and me of an orangutan's belly.

I had always rubbed Lucy's belly during the weeks she lived upstairs, hoping she would continue to let us touch her there. Kit Kat absolutely never allowed such a thing. We took our lives in our hands if we tried. Once when Kit Kat rolled around on her back so that the golden layers of her belly hair gleamed in the sun, she was so fetching that my mother cried out, "Oh, why does she do that if she doesn't want us to touch her tummy?"

But Lucy liked having her belly rubbed, even after being spayed. She got to a point where she would race to meet us in the kitchen and flop down on her back and stretch, a clear invitation to rub her tummy. And everywhere else, for that matter. She liked serious rubbing all over her body. She liked to be petted and scratched, and she liked me to use my fingernails.

At first Joe had feared that Lucy might not be the sharpest knife in the drawer because she had such a knack for getting into trouble. After all, Kit Kat had never gotten into much mischief in the house when she was a teenage kitten. She had matured quickly. But we were still pretty cat-ignorant and needed to understand that curiosity is one way cats display their unique intelligence. We soon saw how very bright Lucy was.

The biggest evidence of this lay in her ways of teaching us games. While Kit Kat ran our lives according to her charming neuroses, Lucy made us play. Always willing to pounce and chase, she would play even in the middle of sheer exhaustion. She needed our interaction to make playtime truly fun for herself, which was rather flattering.

Later I read that Russian Blues are known to teach games to their humans. And it was absolutely true that Lucy managed to dream up all kinds of games Joe and I had never thought of, and somehow she taught them to us. She taught us how to use boxes and paper sacks properly, for one thing. I am fully aware that all cats (except Kit Kat) love boxes and bags, but Lucy had very specific things that were supposed to be done with these, and they had to do with a long wooden spoon.

How she indicated this to me, I cannot say. But when she tucked herself into the bottom of a paper bag or box, I was expected to close the box partway or make certain she was deep inside the bag. If I could see her face, that wouldn't do. She looked right at me with her eyes round and filled with anticipation, and this was my cue to say with great feeling the words, "Cat in a bag!" or "Cat in a box!"

More excitement filled her eyes as she backed down out of my sight. If she took too much time to do this, I was to say, "Go *on*." And she'd scoot out of sight—once more with feeling.

Now I was to scrape the designated wooden spoon along the box corners or the top edges of the bag and make lots of noise. Here came a velvety paw, maybe two of them, grabbing at that spoon, grabbing with an actual grip. Then she'd let go to do it again. And again. And again. And . . . well, you get the picture.

She didn't want to play with the spoon directly. That is, she didn't want me to dangle it in front of her outside the box or bag. Rather, she wanted the spoon to be grab-able while she was inside—grab-able but not easy. There was a touch to this, and I learned it.

This could go on for half an hour if I didn't have other things to do. I egged her on with the noise of the bag or box and sang stupid songs I made up with Lucy's name in them. If anyone had ever heard me, I would have died on the spot of embarrassment. I entertained many guests with this form of play with Lucy—*sans* singing, of course.

For Christmas that year, my sister gave the cats a toy with several long rubber strands that reminded me of miniature automated car wash flaps. Lucy taught me to play through the staircase banister with this specific toy. No other toy would do, so I kept it in the hallway, tucked into a bookshelf. If Lucy saw me head down the hall to the bedroom, and if she was so inclined, she would loop around through the dining and living rooms to get to the foot of the stairs as I approached them from the other direction in the hallway. Then, maintaining eye contact the entire time, she'd race halfway up the stairs, stop, and stare at me through the banister spindles.

This was my cue to turn and grab the toy, then rattle it between the banister spindles, whereupon she would pounce on the rubber strands and chew them, jumping over them and under them. This, too, could go on forever—or at least until Lucy tired. She had bird-like energy—very up-and-at-'em at intense speeds until she wore down, and then there was nothing. She flopped down and went sound asleep just about anywhere.

I had read that Russian Blues are known for playing fetch. Lucy modified the game to something I called *You Fetch*. She was fond of having felt or sisal mice thrown to her so she could give chase, and she preferred this game on linoleum or hardwood so that she could skid, which was half the fun. Once she got hold of the toy mouse, she often managed to toss it up in the air herself and pounce on it again. But other times she would drop the mouse almost immediately and look at me, then away.

I misunderstood this to mean she was bored already. I misunderstood it for several months. But Lucy was patient with me until one day I caught on that dropping the mouse and looking at me was my cue to hurry over, pick the mouse up, and throw it again. *You Fetch*. She ran after it again, pounced, messed around a little, then dropped it, averted her face, and waited for me to repeat the process. We could do this in a circle around the house for who knows how long, wherein I got as much exercise as Lucy.

My very favorite game taught to me by Lucy, however, was a quieter one, and I showed her off with it many times for houseguests. Lucy liked to be held in my arms on her back.

Most of the time that was cuddle time. But sometimes she didn't want to be cuddled exactly. Instead, when I picked her up and placed her on her back, she would stretch her back legs straight out and at the same time stretch her front legs straight back over her head, which hung over my arm. She then splayed all her toes and had me carry her around like that, stretched out to her full length, straight and stiff as a pine log, looking at the world upside down and keeping her balance the whole time.

Now I would chant the Lucy mantra: "Stretching is happiness . . . Stretching is happiness . . ." As she held this pose, I learned to head for the stairs or a jutting corner or any high piece of furniture with items on it.

Now I said, "Grab. Grab . . ." At which point Lucy would stretch out over her head and grab the banister spindles with her paws, watching them, upside down of course. Or she would grab a corner we were rounding. Or books on the higher shelves of the bookcases. Or knickknacks. Or anything else that she could reach from this height in my arms. Anytime I said, "Grab," she grabbed. This game truly was a crowd-pleaser.

It occurred to me that probably she would grab even if I didn't say the word. After all, she dreamed this game up in the first place. But I never tested it. I didn't want to know.

With such a playful personality, Lucy had that knack for getting into mischief, but it only seemed to happen when we were home. That's when she came alive and scampered about or jumped in the air with excitement or did a coyote dance. Though we didn't catch on right away, Joe and I came to recognize that this frolicking happened when she wanted our attention. Kit Kat was not this way. When she wanted our attention, she simply locked eyes with us and bee-lined in our direction. Lucy was less direct about it.

With my work, I was away from home at least three nights a month, and sometimes I was gone for a week or more. If I was gone more than one night consecutively, Lucy would not let me anywhere near her when I first came home, though she usually came around by bedtime. If I was gone a week, however, it was usually twenty-four hours before I could touch her. She liked playing with Joe, but Russian Blues tend to imprint on their preferred human, and I was that human. So I must be punished.

This meant that upon my return, she would stay just out of reach and watch me, but I was not to approach her. If I did, she gave me a horrified look and scooted to where I couldn't reach her but where she could still keep her eye on me. This actually induced guilt in me until I learned that this was all simply a ritual that must be performed.

Once when I had been gone for a total of ten days, an all-time high, I gave up trying to make nice. I parked myself on the bed and watched the late news. I began to have that feeling that I was being watched. I looked around, and sure enough, Lucy sat under the vanity, staring at me. From that distance, eye contact was fine, and we stared at each other for a while as I cooed and coaxed, to no avail. She would not budge.

I sighed and went back to the television. Pretty soon, I scooted down in the bed and watched the news. Lucy couldn't see my face. I glanced at the vanity again. Lucy had picked herself up and repositioned herself so she could see my face. There she sat, staring at me once again.

Somehow Joe discovered that, at such times, if he put Lucy

in a box and put the box next to me, she would let me touch her. In fact, I could rub any part of her body and pet her and tickle her and even kiss her as long as she was in a box. While I made a fuss over her, she wouldn't budge. She wouldn't purr, either, but she let me touch her while she averted her eyes. After a couple days, she would let me hold her again.

Of course Kit Kat watched this interaction. She observed that her sister received a great deal of attention any time she hopped into the dreaded box. One day when we played with Lucy in a box in the kitchen, I turned to see that Kit Kat had quietly put herself into a low-sided box, the kind that cases of soda come in. There she sat, staring not at us but straight ahead. She looked so uncomfortable. But it was as if she were saying, "See? I'm fun too." Joe picked her up and cuddled her. We assured her she needn't do that again, and she never did.

Fortunately in the many hours Joe and I were away from home, the two cats were good company to each other. As Lucy and Kit Kat forged a relationship, I came to believe they could not have been better sisters had they come from the same litter. Lucy was kind of pesky with Kit Kat, and Kit Kat was bossy and territorial with Lucy. But the two of them got along well most of the time. I usually came home before Joe, and if the cats didn't meet me at the door, it was likely I'd find them taking their siesta together in the bedroom, curled around each other like yin and yang.

What knocked us out, however, was that these two cats showed concern for each other. The first time we ever heard Kit Kat hacking over a hairball that had trouble making its appearance, Joe and I held her on the couch and fussed over her. Pretty soon Lucy galloped in from out of nowhere and hustled onto our laps with what seemed to me to be a worried look. Kit Kat turned to her, and they made eye contact. Then Kit Kat hacked gently, and Lucy slowly reached her face down to Kit Kat's face. They touched noses. It seemed very tender. Lucy sat and waited until Kit Kat stopped hacking, and then Lucy romped off.

One time I came home after having been gone twelve hours. Joe was not yet home from work, and I was met at the door by a highly agitated Kit Kat. She yowled all through my unlocking, something she hadn't done since pre-Lucy days. And there was no Lucy at the door with her.

I spoke to Kit Kat as I put down my things, and I asked her where Lucy was, feeling for all the world like little Timmy saying to a barking Lassie, "What's wrong, girl? *What?* Someone fell down the abandoned mine shaft?"

Kit Kat stomped through the kitchen, then looked back to see if I was following. (I was.) She continued down the hall. She stopped at the bedroom door and looked up at me. The door was tightly shut. I had left Lucy on the bed that morning with the door wide open. What happened? And was Lucy still inside?

She certainly was, and probably had been all day. We had recently installed new windows, and I was not yet used to them. When I left the house that day, I had left the windows lowered from the top. They worked like transom windows, letting in wonderful cross breezes. But I realized now that the breezes this day were wind gusts that slammed the bedroom door shut.

Lucy was parked right at the threshold, and she was mighty glad to see me. But first she and Kit Kat stopped and touched noses. Now all was well.

Of course they didn't always get along, especially once Lucy was an adult. They had their house cat spats. Once when our vet was handling the good-natured Lucy, she asked me, "Is Lucy submissive to Kit Kat?"

There was no doubt in anyone's mind at the vet clinic that Kit Kat was dominant. But was Lucy submissive?

"Not exactly," I said. The correct word was *deferential*. Lucy deferred to Kit Kat, and only when she wanted to. The fact that it was most of the time had more to do with Lucy's irritation than Kit Kat's dominance. Lucy tolerated Kit Kat's aggressiveness with that unbelievable scowl Lucy could get on her face, and when she didn't want the hassle anymore, she walked away. Unless she didn't want to walk away. Then Miss Lucy wasn't all that cooperative. And let the games begin!

Sometimes when the two cats had their confrontations, Lucy kick-boxed. Based on some communication Joe and I could never follow, the two would lock eyes suddenly and freeze. Then Kit Kat slowly crouched and growled, ears flat. Lucy maintained eye contact and slowly, slowly, turned the back end of her body toward Kit Kat, never taking her eyes off her. Joe and I were reminded of the Three Stooges in *Niagara Falls* ("Slowly I turn. . . .").

Now a back leg kicked out at Kit Kat. Once, twice, several times, like something from a Bruce Lee movie. On occasion, Lucy flopped on her back and kicked like a kangaroo. Most of the time Kit Kat sparred, and the two looked like little bears cuffing each other. Sometimes, however, Kit Kat looked kind of freaked-out, and she would slink out of the room.

Though usually Kit Kat had the upper hand with Lucy in such times, sometimes Kit Kat seemed very anxious instead. Joe and I never could understand what caused which response. We figured it wasn't serious, since Lucy was pretty benign when you came right down to it. We knew our Kit Kat had her issues.

But Lucy had only one "issue." I noticed that when the wind was particularly fierce—and our winds off the plain many times took out the electricity, sometimes for a couple of days—she appeared anxious. Joe and I believed that Lucy had not been outside in that windchill more than the one day on which we met her, and we assumed that whatever fear she had felt out there had dissipated from her memory long ago.

But when winds hit the house from the flat southwest fields and whistled and whined around the corners of the house, I thought otherwise. I would see Lucy hunker down in the middle of the southwest dining room floor and watch the long windows, one by one. Sitting on a hardwood floor in the middle of a room was not typical behavior for our high-places cat.

On these occasions, I would speak to Lucy, and she would turn her face to me. I saw what I believed to be a little trepidation and even a little sadness in her eyes. I would speak soothingly to her, but it didn't seem to help. She would turn back to her study of the scary noises.

But most of the time, Lucy was pretty non-neurotic. Her demands in life were made gently, and her curiosity usually overcame whatever reticence she felt over new things. I saw this with children. We had no children, and children seldom had occasion to come to our house. Neither cat had ever met a child until we hired a housecleaner who one day brought her five-year-old son, Blake, with her.

Blake loved animals, and he wanted to play with ours. At first, the cats observed him from beneath a buffet while he tried to lure them out. They had never before seen such a small human, and they clearly did not know what to make of him. They stared and stared, keeping their distance. I thought they looked at him as if they thought there might be something very wrong with him that made him little.

When Blake's mom fired up the vacuum sweeper, Kit Kat headed under the bed for the rest of the afternoon. So Blake concentrated on Lucy. We broke out the toys, and Lucy simply could not help herself. If this diminutive human was going to play, well by golly, so was she. I credit Blake for getting Lucy over her shyness with children. Kit Kat came around eventually, but she would never actually play with him or with other children.

And it was all just in time for a summertime visit from Joe's family. His parents, two sisters, one brother-in-law, and two small nieces piled in from New York for three days of humid, ninety-plus degree weather, and I had such a wonderful time with them that I cried watching them drive away. The little girls, Colleen and Meaghan, fell in love with Lucy. They only saw Kit Kat once when she chose to receive visitors in the bedroom. The rest of the time she stayed under the bed until the girls had gone upstairs for the night.

But Lucy played and played. She played into exhaustion all day, every day. She would not leave the kitchen, the center of all activity, unless we were on the patio. Then she'd sit on the other side of the window screen to watch the girls' every move. At night, she slept so hard I could pick up her paw and drop it and she never budged. I could do this over and over. Then in the morning, she parked herself where the girls would know she was ready to play again. She was like a drunk on a three-day binge.

The little girls adored her. Colleen took one of my favorite snapshots of Lucy in the window, and Meaghan couldn't get enough of playing with Lucy any more than Lucy could get enough play.

At the end of the second day at our house, my sister-in-law asked Meaghan what her favorite part of Michigan was. She said, "Aunt Lonnie." At that, I puffed up like a puffer fish.

On the last day of their visit, my sister-in-law again asked Meaghan what her favorite part of Michigan was.

This time she said, "Lucy."

·11·

THE GREAT INDOORS

The smallest feline is a masterpiece.
Leonardo da Vinci

Kit Kat and Lucy were full-time indoor cats. From the time they came to live with us, they were never again allowed outdoors. On the one hand, I knew it kept them safe. On the other hand, I knew these little beasts were created to run and climb, so I felt guilty keeping them indoors.

The cats I grew up with could come and go as they pleased. In the old family farmhouse where I grew up, my folks chose not to repair the broken basement window so that our indoor-outdoor cats could go outside for potty time and come back indoors for shelter. They would make their way up from the basement by climbing uneven basement stairs made of stone, crossing a utility room at the top, and pawing open a door to the kitchen, a door which never fully closed. It was a nice setup.

Since my family home had five acres of lawn and gardens and was surrounded by additional acres and acres of woods, fields, and swamps, the roaming and hunting potential for cats was truly enviable. The road was only moderately traveled in those days. My stepdad cut out the first cat door I ever saw in his workshop in an enclosed barn some distance from the house, so our cats were further protected from the elements while exploring away from the house.

After college, I lived a couple of decades without cats, and I didn't know until we got Kit Kat that current wisdom says cats should be kept indoors for their health and safety. Before we knew this, Joe and I were already keeping Kit Kat indoors for three reasons—the horrible truck traffic outside, her alleged contagious FIP, and my own anxiety. Nevertheless, I felt guilty about what I was raised to believe would be imprisonment for animals who wanted to experience the great outdoors.

But then I read in many sources that keeping a cat indoors extended its life by four years, so those were four more good reasons not to feel guilty about things. I read other variations on that statistic—one being that an indoor male cat who is neutered and well-cared-for has a life expectancy of sixteen to seventeen years. Indoor females can live seventeen to nineteen years. But the average life expectancy for an outdoor cat is only three to five years. I can attest to those numbers. My childhood cats seldom lived longer than three years.

Kit Kat did not seem to mind being indoors. She had had a stressful life as a feral. The only time she actually hung around waiting for a door to open was when we had Alberta the hen living in the yard. Otherwise, Kit Kat stayed away from the doors when we came and went.

Of course if doors were open for any length of time, she was naturally curious. One time she wandered outside when some workers left the back door open. I saw the open door and ran outside. Fortunately I found her just a few feet away, tucked into my kitchen garden, chewing on tomato leaves. I was relieved almost to the point of tears that she hadn't headed for the fields, or worse, the road. I started growing oat grass indoors for her from that point on.

Lucy did not rush the doors. She spent most of her time sitting on windowsills watching birds and small creatures. Or else she ran from window to window with a noisy, brisk trot that I came to recognize as Lucy On The Move. Lucy was the first cat I ever heard make chirping and clicking sounds in her mouth, what I'm told is the sound of frustration for house cats who cannot give chase. It sort of broke my heart, because I knew she wanted to stretch her legs and run across the fields.

But I knew that Lucy running outdoors would mean Lucy running across the road, and without a doubt that would mean Lucy getting killed. If I was going to have to worry about these cats I loved getting killed, I could not have cats.

When I was a child, while our cats certainly had The Life, they also got into serious trouble in the outdoors. I worried about them all the time. More than one of my beloved cats was killed by traffic. Other times, my cat would be gone for days, then drag itself home beaten-up by another creature. Fluffy #2 left the house one morning and I never saw her again. Every night I wondered if my cats would come home, and I would call for them over and over at the back door. I was sick to my stomach each and every night until they showed up. To have to worry about their lives was torture for me.

But in those days, that's how things were done; nobody I knew kept a cat exclusively indoors, not counting Boots' previous owner. Everyone I knew understood that cats were wild animals pretending not to be—and that's true enough. But the general belief then was that it would be cruel to keep such an animal indoors. People lived with the risks of losing their pet outdoors, and because I had no choice in childhood, so did I.

I don't recall the contagious cat diseases being prevalent back then. In the late seventies, our ginger male died of feline leukemia, but he was old. I don't recall the vet telling us it was contagious—we had another cat at the time, so it seems like she should have been tested, but she wasn't. Years later, when Joe and I were given Kit Kat's false diagnosis of FIP, I'd never heard of that disease. The fact that she allegedly had contracted it from other cats made the outdoors more dangerous than ever.

It helped when Joe and I came to realize our cats were living a wonderful life inside our home. The house was big and airy, for one thing, and the main rooms ran in a circle with a staircase, all of which was perfect for the cats to run and leap and chase each other. We made pathways under the bed, perfect for tunneling and hiding. The house was cat-proofed and safe; Joe even secured our tall bookcases on the old uneven floors so that the fearless Lucy could leap up and roam on them safely.

We had lots of long windows with no drapes and only a couple of hanging shades, so the cats had plenty of fresh air when the windows were open, in addition to lots of light all year, by which these one-time desert creatures could sun themselves. Kit Kat followed the sun in the course of a day. She started out sleeping off breakfast in the east bedroom, moved to the south mudroom around noon for the big afternoon siesta, and finally napped lightly in the west rooms as she waited for Joe to come home from work, at which point she woke right up.

Lucy stayed glued to windows most of the time, any and all of them, according to the whims of house finches out there. Or squirrels, rabbits, and wild turkeys. On humid nights with all those windows open, it could feel like we were outside. Then both cats sat long into the night on the wide windowsills, watching the dark, their noses twitching.

We eventually acquired a 6'3" carpeted cat tower from a local feed store. This was designed by someone who clearly understood cats. It had ledges, ropes, pillars to scratch, two round beds, and two hollow kiosks, plus it was freestanding, a necessary feature due to our high ceilings. It was far superior to anything I have ever seen in a pet store. We placed it in our only south window. I always laughed about the fact that I—a person who has always enjoyed furnishing my home with yard sale finds—spent more money on the cat tower than I did on my couch.

Once the cats adjusted to this behemoth and claimed their territories on it, they spent a good part of their day there. They climbed it, played fort on it, dangled from it, slept on it, and stopped clawing other things in favor of clawing the tower. From what I could see, it provided the exercise potential of a feline fitness gym, and both cats actually trimmed down a little once they had the tower.

About the time Lucy came to us, I was reading a book

called *The Tribe of Tiger* by Elizabeth Marshall Thomas, the author of the more widely read bestseller, *The Hidden Life of Dogs*. Thomas was an anthropologist who became interested in the big cats of Africa when she did fieldwork there. Her book talks about the ways in which all cats—big, small, wild, domestic—share behaviors and why.

Thomas says that, in her opinion, a circus cat—if owned by a loving trainer—lives a relatively happy life. She knows this isn't a popular opinion, but she believes circus cats have a far happier life than do cats in zoos. Besides the fact that regular food and shelter lessen any animal's stress, circus cats get to do two things cats of all sizes love to do: watch and play. They watch the lively activities of the circus from their cages, and at some point every single day, they get out and interact with someone who will focus on them and play with them. It's a huge ritualistic pleasure for any cat.

Although big cats in the circus are not something I care to watch, reading that made me start to relax about Kit Kat and Lucy's indoor life. Certainly our cats were less cooped up than circus cats, plus they were well-fed, vaccinated, entertained, and adored. I needed to stop wishing they could go outside and instead be glad their life was full and relatively free of unnecessary stress. Besides, contagious feline diseases had become that other compelling reason to keep the girls from going out. Our new vet also endorsed keeping the girls indoors.

Any vet would like the easygoing Lucy; however, Kit Kat was more of an acquired taste. She was difficult to handle on the examining table—so difficult that I suspected our new vet—a local country doctor we found after leaving the clinic that misdiagnosed Kit Kat—actually didn't like her.

He was a guy who showed up for Saturday morning appointments wearing camouflage and who had a deer trophy on his clinic wall, a buck I assumed he bagged himself. I wondered if maybe he wasn't a warm fuzzy kind of guy about pets.

A matter-of-fact approach to animals is not unusual in old-school vets. The field of veterinary medicine was not originally about keeping pets, after all. It was about keeping farm animals alive and well for the sake of a food source and livelihood. Ailing animals meant loss of income and loss of food for farm families. Pet expert Donna remembered that back in the sixties, her veterinarian father had taken some flak from other vets in the state when he started a solely small animal practice.

Keeping cats as house pets in particular is a fairly modern thing. For rural people, cats were working animals—barn mousers who produced litter after litter of cats to do the job, and if some of those cats died, well, there would be more soon enough.

The hunter-vet really liked Lucy. Who wouldn't? She was just easy. We didn't believe in declawing, but this vet tried on many occasions to get us to change our minds, especially regarding Miss Kit Kat, who rarely kept her claws retracted. He told us his own cats were declawed and they were fine. That was the only way he could live with them, he said.

But Joe and I had learned that declawing is debilitating to a cat. It's like taking off a human's fingertip to the first knuckle. Some cats don't do well with it at all, especially older cats. We chose to deal with our cats' claws by having them trimmed every few weeks, a procedure much like how we humans trim our own toenails. Simple.

Well, it should have been simple. Unfortunately, Kit Kat

did not like to have her feet touched at all. She would be stoically silent during an injection, but touch a paw? Oh no. She hissed and growled through the entire claw-trimming procedure every single time. Until the day she screamed. Oh, yes. She screamed bloody murder.

I wasn't there when it happened because we had a houseguest, and I admit that I thought Joe was being dramatic when he reported it to me later. He said Kit Kat had started out with her usual hissing and growling, but by the second paw, her vocalizing had turned into screaming.

That day the vet put down his nail clippers for good. He told Joe he would not trim Kit Kat's claws anymore. He said he was afraid someone—we assume he meant himself—was going to get hurt. He again pitched declawing to Joe.

But we were not going to declaw Kit Kat. Yes, she was quick to use her claws. She didn't even play without claws extended. But we simply would not maim her. We decided our furniture wasn't that important. We took care when we played with her, watched her expressive tail for clues, and kept peroxide available for when we missed the clues and got swiped.

By the time the vet pitched us one last time on declawing, Kit Kat was too neurotic, too set in her ways, and too prone to acting out for anyone to consider such an operation. We were surprised the vet didn't see that.

So when Joe brought The Screamer home that day and reported the doctor's line in the sand, he added, "You know, if he won't trim her nails, what else won't he do?"

Good point. I said that I had always had the feeling this vet didn't like Kit Kat. Our houseguest looked at me in amazement and said, "Why would you take your cat to someone who doesn't like her?"

Another good point. Embarrassing, really, that someone would even have to ask it. We decided to look for another vet.

In the meantime, Donna paid us another visit to teach us how to trim Kit Kat's claws at home. She showed us her technique on Lucy first and suggested we always do this work in the same spot on the kitchen counter. "Grab the cat as she's walking by," she said, "plop her up here, cut her nails, shut up while you're doing it, and then put her back where you picked her up. The cat should at that point look around and think, *What just happened?*"

Donna herself was as smooth as silk trimming Kit Kat. No screaming there. And we could do Lucy ourselves—who couldn't? All Lucy would do was avert her pretty face during the procedure. But Joe and I came away realizing we absolutely could not and would not trim Kit Kat's nails at home. Not if we valued our own skin.

A few weeks later, Kit Kat vomited a horrendous foreign object—a wide, flat piece of ribbon. Cats are known to ingest linear objects, but I'd never known Kit Kat to do that, so I was perplexed by it. I eventually theorized that she had probably tried to play with the ribbon and then couldn't get it off her (by then) way-too-long claws without chewing at it. This had probably led her to start swallowing it, and then she had to continue. However it had happened, it made her very sick. Our hunter vet was on vacation, so we were forced to find another vet immediately.

My ophthalmologist had expensive hunting dogs. He swore by a certain rural clinic about ten miles from us, claiming they had "the second best dog man in the state." This of course begged the question as to where the first was, his response being Michigan State University, known for its veterinary school and sometimes called Moo U. Joe and I wondered if the second best dog man in the state might also be a cat man. It turned out that he was, and so was she, the other vet at the clinic. When we called, they said they could take us right away, so we bundled up the ailing Kit Kat and headed out.

The road to the clinic was a back road, and while driving it, we came upon a railroad crossing. There were no lights or gate at this track—just a sign that read "Yield." Take a minute and think about that.

At the clinic, we were greeted in the lobby by two old cats who lived in the clinic full-time, including Ricky, a white male who liked to drape himself over visiting cat carriers. We took that as a positive sign.

Indeed, the doctors and staff dealt beautifully with Kit Kat right away. She hissed and growled, of course, but they worked around it. They were so good with Kit Kat that Joe and I looked at each other in the silent hope they might be willing to trim her claws. Finally we dared to ask, and they said they'd be happy to.

The vets and techs were refreshingly philosophical about Kit Kat's personality. This was the first time I actually heard her scream, and the sound of my cat so upset sort of broke my heart.

But the vet and techs yelled merrily over the horror. "We see worse all the time," they said, to which I wondered why they stayed in the profession. I was very glad they *had* stayed in it, however, because it took three of them working together to do the deed, during which Joe and I obsessively apologized. They tried a technique of wrapping a towel around Kit Kat's head except for her face, and that seemed to help a little. They were fast like Donna, and soon enough, it was over.

Afterward, the vet scratched the top of Kit Kat's head and assured us that all was fine. "Your cat is not trying to hurt us," he said. "She just wants us to stop, and she's expressive about it." He continued to scratch the spot over and between Kit Kat's eyes. "You know," he continued, "if we judge people by their color, of course we're racist. But we *can* judge cats by their color. She's a three-colored cat, and they are . . ." he paused, "independent."

How kind.

To say Joe and I were relieved over this turn of events in our vet world is a huge understatement. We were positively giddy, and we immediately made an appointment for Lucy to have a checkup and a nail trim the following week. After that we took both cats in every month for nail trims, and though Kit Kat still resorted to screaming, she did it less quickly. The techs made it a challenge to get through a trim without Kit Kat screaming. One of them told us, "It's like watching a scary movie where you know something's going to jump out and scare you. You just don't know when."

I felt bad that Kit Kat was unable to put her best paw forward at this vet clinic, especially since everyone there was so good to her. At our house, Kit Kat really liked people, even strangers. Lucy, on the other hand, was shy, hiding whenever someone new came into the house. But visitors were all greeted at the door by the hospitable Kit Kat. We called her The Social Director. She would look straight into the eyes of our guests, jump in their laps, and purr. When my mother and sister and others whose scent she recognized came to visit, she almost gushed with happiness.

So during one screaming session at the vet clinic, I felt compelled to tell the techs, "I want you to know that as difficult as this cat is, she is also that sweet, and you never get to see that." I told them how cuddly she was, like a living teddy bear. They assured me they believed me.

Nevertheless, I was glad that during a later hospitalization, Kit Kat won the clinic staff over. Apparently after about twenty-four hours on an IV, Kit Kat felt more like her best self and determined she'd need to turn on the charm. She kicked in her purr, and she stuck her pink tongue out partway and held it there, another charming habit of hers.

Once Kit Kat the Lover showed herself, it was a turning point for everyone. While the staff had always been kind to Kit Kat, I noticed they referred to her as "sweetie" after that and petted her more. At the same time, the staff won Kit Kat over too. At least she screamed less. The day actually came when sometimes claw-trimming resulted in no screaming at all. Sometimes.

Lucy was another story altogether. She was a little freaked-out by the vet's office, which was not helped by her sister's vocalizing, and this made Lucy a tad squirmy. But always gentle. Trimming Lucy became the reward for our very patient vets and techs after they trimmed Kit Kat. Lucy's only expression of displeasure during trimming was to avert her face. I didn't even have to put her on the table. The trimming was done paw by paw as I held her in my arms.

Although we were pleased with this vet clinic, one time they sent home the wrong drops for Lucy's ears. The drops actually wouldn't "drop"—they slimed instead. Lucy was absolutely beside herself at this grainy, sticky gel-like substance that was in her ears and down her fur below her ears. She would not let me near her for quite a while. I read on the container that it was for dogs only, so I called the clinic and complained not only about the wrong med but about how it was upsetting my cat. They offered to clean her up.

I drove Lucy back to the vet. I set down her carrier in the lobby and stepped into the powder room. When I came out, she'd been whisked away without a word. Odd, but I wasn't concerned.

Until she returned. She was soaking wet and looked like a rat. They put her in her carrier like that, and now I needed to take her out in chilly March weather.

When we got back to the house, I towel-dried her. It appeared that no actual cleaning of her ears and the fur under them had taken place, only apparently some kind of hosing down. I was very unhappy about this, and so was Lucy. She needed a true cleaning.

Could I bathe a cat?

Not only had I never bathed a cat in my life, I'd never even considered the need to. At the time, there were no YouTube videos to help me. But I thought about how Lucy didn't mind being lightly sprayed from open windows in rain; she didn't hate water. I thought about how she liked a rough texture to sit on, so I worked with that knowledge. I lined the small bathroom sink with a wet and warm nubby washcloth. I remembered a Canadian woman who once told me any time you're going to do something new with a cat, tell the cat first. So I held Lucy next to the sink and said, "Momma's going to have to clean your fur. Will you let me?" She looked in my eyes, then away. I took it to mean, "Go ahead . . . if you must . . ."

I set Lucy on the warm, wet washcloth in the sink basin. She seemed to like it. The sink basin was small and round, the kind of thing she would like to snuggle into. I ran warm tap water gently, and I poured cups of it over her body, then over the sides of her head. No problem. I applied a little bit of baby shampoo (I would use Dawn dishwashing liquid next time), sudsed up her fur, and rinsed, talking to her in soothing tones. She simply sat and stared straight ahead until I was finished. It felt like when she allowed me to pet her all over as long as she was sitting in a box.

Then came bliss for Lucy—I toweled her off with warm, rough towels. Oh, she loved that. Let the purring begin! She seemed to appreciate that her fur had come clean. A little too perfume-y, but clean. I think Lucy understood I was trying to help her.

Joe and I came to believe that Kit Kat and Lucy were gifts personally delivered to us, one by one, to help us settle into our big house in the middle of nowhere. We had not known we needed these cats, and we would never have sought them out. Rather, they had had to show up at our very door and ask to live with us.

We cherished these little felines entrusted to our care. And the beauty of it was that they took care of us right back, in their own way, in their own time. They became wonderful companions for us. They were barometers for our emotions. They comforted us when we were tired or frightened or ill. They had ways of letting us know they did not like us to be stressed. They got us to stay home, relax, take naps, play. We came to wonder what we ever did without them.

It was the otherwise macho Ernest Hemingway with his talent for uncluttered language who made this surprising statement: "I have just one consolation in my life. My kitty."

I would not try to say it better than that.

·12·

ALL CREATURES

A cat is more intelligent than people
believe, and can be taught any crime.

Mark Twain

An old farmhouse is bound to have critters living in it—
critters other than the ones who were invited to live there,
that is. Growing up in a Michigan farmhouse built in 1835
by my great-great-grandfather, I shared my home with any
number of uninvited mice, squirrels, raccoons, birds, and
rabbits who made their way indoors. Often these critters
wound up behind the walls or in the attic, and we could hear
them scratching or mewling.

My folks had that broken basement window so that the
cats could come and go as they pleased, which meant any

other four-legged creature could come and go as well. Even an occasional snake in the basement was not unusual.

When I was a senior in high school, a screech owl found its way into the house, and I woke up one Sunday morning to find him sitting on the fireplace hearth, eyeballing me. My folks were away for the weekend and I was alone, so I considered my options. I certainly didn't want the poor thing to start flying around indoors. Rumor had it that firemen would fetch cats from trees. Would they be willing to get an owl out of a house? I called the local fire department.

The township fire department was a volunteer one. They had recently bought a new fire truck, and here it came, roaring down the road, three volunteer firemen in full gear on board, even though I had been very clear on the phone that there was no fire. They all clomped inside the house and checked out the situation.

The captain laughed and donned a pair of heavy gloves. He approached the owl, picked it up without a fuss, walked outside, and let it go. Then the men hopped back on their snappy new fire truck and roared away. This took all of sixty seconds.

More often we had mice in my family home. Most farmhouses have them, and we knew we had them because they left their scat here and there, which my mother referred to with great disgust as "mouse doings." We found those "doings" every now and then in baking pans, over sweaters in drawers, between folded towels. This meant more work for us getting things clean again. Mice were a nuisance for which my parents had no patience, and in my folks' house, mice were poisoned. I hated poison, and I wouldn't use it when it was my turn to deal with house mice. How can you poison mice if you've ever seen a Disney movie?

When I was on my own in a basement apartment, I was one time overrun with mice. I tried ignoring them, hoping they'd move on. But it got so they wouldn't even take cover when I walked in the room. I tried traps, but the apartment had only two rooms, so when the mouse got snapped I just couldn't take it, especially if death was not immediate. The first time it happened and woke me up, I called my night-owl boyfriend on the phone. "Shut your bedroom door," he advised. "It will be over soon."

The next night while I slept, a mouse slid down a buttered popcorn bowl sitting in the sink with a few inches of water in it. Come morning, I found Mr. Mouse belly-up in the water. That seemed pretty painless—or at least it was silent—so that was my trap of choice for a while—a mixing bowl donated to the cause with buttered sides and water in the bottom. I actually caught a mouse per day that way for several days. Then I'd take mouse and water and throw it all on my garden's compost pile. I guess the word got back to Mouseville, because they stopped showing up.

In our Moscow house, prior to the arrival of Kit Kat, Joe and I were on occasion overrun with mice, necessitating our using traps, something it turned out Joe disliked as much as I. We decided against using the "friendly" traps that allow you to release the mouse outside; they were coming right back in, and who had time for all that? At least the snap-traps were fast. But we hated them.

Enter Kit Kat. Nature can be cruel, but it does work. We decided to allow Kit Kat to do whatever hunting she chose to do when she moved indoors and to give her free rein to do what came naturally. I say "allow" as if we had any choice in the matter. All cats are natural-born killers. They fool us with their cuddly, adorable ways and manage to make us forget how fierce they really are.

But cats are obligate carnivores. Cats will literally die if they cannot eat the flesh of other creatures, so their instinct is to hunt and kill. Even a cat's play is all about hunting, pouncing, and killing anything that moves. Mother cats right away teach their babies the moves for killing prey, helping them fine-tune those natural instincts so that those babies will grow up able to find food. And no matter how well-fed a cat is, she will hunt if the situation presents itself. Elizabeth Marshall Thomas begins her book, *The Tribe of Tiger*, with: "The story of cats is a story of meat. . . ."[*]

When Kit Kat was a teenage kitten, we used to show off her ferocity to our guests with a toy that had a *faux* mouse at the end of a wire. "Watch," Joe would say. "Two moves: one pounce, one bite to the neck." Indeed, Kit Kat would pounce on the gray flannel object, bite its *faux* neck one time, then sit back and look at us as if to say, "My work here is done."

So when Kit Kat came indoors to live with us, Joe and I agreed we would stop trapping and give mice a sporting chance. At the same time, Kit Kat could get some exercise doing what she was engineered to do. There is that folk wisdom that says that having the scent of a cat in the house keeps mice away, but I've yet to see it. We always had monster-sized cats in the house I grew up in, and we always had plenty more mice than cats. What I *have* seen is a mouse sitting right down to nibble a meal in the very same room with a cat who hasn't noticed it.

*Elizabeth Marshall Thomas, *The Tribe of Tiger* (New York: Simon and Schuster, 1994), 17.

But Kit Kat noticed. When she did, Joe and I quietly left the room. Most times we would find the mouse corpse in the kitchen, though one morning we woke up to find blood on our bed and a mouse head next to it. Only the head.

When Lucy arrived, Kit Kat taught her how to hunt. There's no other way to put it. As a kitten, Lucy knew enough to pounce, but then she seemed a little bewildered. At that point, Kit Kat would move in and take over while Lucy watched. Kit Kat's intensity at hunting sometimes kept her glued to one spot for hours at a time while Lucy scampered off on her merry way to some other fun thing. This was the case until Lucy matured. Then she, too, became a formidable hunter.

Around that time I read that, like big cats in the wild, domestic cats—even housebound ones—team hunt. I hadn't known that, since my childhood cats were indoor-outdoor. Once I was alerted to it, I observed that this was the case with Kit Kat and Lucy.

Eventually they got so adept at working together that it looked like all their hunting was done in tandem. One would corner the mouse while the other watched from a short distance. When the first cat flushed out the mouse, the second cat pounced. They would relay as needed. That's as much as I cared to watch, but I maintain it's better than trapping or poisoning. Fortunately, new basement windows stopped the steady inflow of mice at our house, and it became rare to see evidence of mice and even rarer to see an actual mouse.

And then one day Lucy was given a mouse straight from the heavens.

My office was the farmhouse mudroom, where the working men of former days would come inside and take off their manure-encrusted boots on really ugly linoleum. Measuring only a hundred square feet in size, our mudroom was truly a small hub of the house for us, almost a little rotary with doors leading to the kitchen, the bathroom, the basement, Joe's office, and the back door—no kidding. The mudroom also had a nice south window where the cats chose to hang out and where we placed the tall cat tower.

It seemed that the previous owner of the house had spent no money he didn't have to spend, which was both good news and bad news. Unlike most Michigan farmhouses, our solid brick house had gone through very little trendy remodeling on the outside. It had no attached garage, no family room addition, no huge picture windows. The owner before the previous one had added a patio to the side and a portico to the front probably in the late 1940s, but that was all. They looked good, and if someone wanted to be a purist about restoration, these could be removed without scarring the outside of the house.

Inside the house was a mixed bag of tasteful remodeling from that same time—coved ceilings, arched doorways, oak hardwood floors—and truly ugly remodeling from the 1960s–70s—dark fake-wood paneling, three different kinds of *faux* tile in the downstairs bathroom, lots of badly lowered ceilings. One of the upstairs rooms had dark paneling showing images of duck hunters—the same ones over and over all around the room.

My mudroom office had the worst of the bad remodeling. Its phenomenally ugly paneling had been put on the walls in sawed-up pieces, and it was scratched and scarred and bowing out in some places. It looked like drunks did the work.

In many nineteenth-century farmhouses, bathrooms were added later, and this was true in ours. On the first floor, the only bathroom was under the back staircase and next to the back door of the house. This meant that the bathroom door was situated in such a way that if it was almost shut but not quite, you couldn't open the back door from the outside. Nor could you get out of the bathroom if someone didn't completely shut the back door. The joys of the old house experience.

For some reason, in the lowered ceiling right in front of the back door and bathroom door, a square hole had been cut that measured around four inches by four inches. Maybe a cable had been threaded up there for some reason, though I could never imagine why.

Lucy was about a year old when she strolled into the mudroom one day while I was working at the computer. She sat down at the back door and watched the threshold.

"Whatcha doing, Lucy?" I asked her. She looked at me and squawked, her way of acknowledging her name. Then she went back to studying the threshold. I wondered if she heard or smelled a mouse in the enclosed back porch. I figured if she stayed there very long, I'd let her into the porch to see what she could see. I went back to my typing, glancing at her from time to time.

After about ten minutes, I turned again to Lucy, who still watched the threshold. I heard a noise in the ceiling and looked up just in time to see a mouse drop through the cut-out square straight to the floor. It landed right at Lucy's feet.

Lucy pulled back in surprise and stared at the mouse, which had landed on its back and was stunned into immobility. Then she reached down, picked it up with her mouth, and trotted out of the room. I never before or since knew a mouse to fall from the ceiling, and Lucy never planted herself in that spot again. I have since been amazed at the olfactory sense of cats, and I can only imagine she smelled something and decided to wait for it to appear. Still, it seemed like the heavens favored Lucy that day.

So our cats hunted in our house. And because our cats hunted indoors only, we were never faced with them bringing us "gifts" of birds or rabbits, dead or alive. Mice were their game, and that was it.

Until the bat.

Most of my bat experience came from attending movies as a child at the since-torn-down Family Theatre in downtown Jackson, Michigan. This old venue could always be counted on to have bats crisscrossing through the air in front of the big glowing screen. We kids were excited when that happened, screaming and laughing at the same time.

I was told that bats lived under the shutters at my childhood home, but I rarely saw them. In fact, I never saw a bat up close until Joe and I moved into our farmhouse. We heard them, we saw them, we shooed them out of upstairs windows. We hesitated to have company stay over because of them, since the bats for the most part made appearances only upstairs where we were fixing up guest rooms.

But Joe and I met our final house bat on a more intimate level one early spring morning, the very week we had been discussing blowing insulation into the attic and possibly between the walls. We'd never been up in the attic, and we weren't sure if there was space between the bricks in the walls, so we didn't know if there was insulation anywhere in the house.

But we did know we needed insulation for the next winter. The previous winter's heating bills had just about done us in, and it didn't help that our propane gas company was under investigation by attorneys general in three states.

Added to this was the fact that the windows and storm windows were in horrible shape when we moved in. Most of them wouldn't open at all, and they all had leaks around the framing. One window in the upstairs southwest corner room was so bad the wind literally blew the curtains hanging at that closed window all winter. I had heard stories from my parents about how when they were children during the Great Depression, they would wake up to snow drifts on the windowsills. Now sometimes so did I.

We switched propane companies, and that helped. But we planned to reduce that heat bill even more with insulation, and we made an appointment with a local handyman to come over and check things out.

That week, I woke up on a dark morning to the smell of coffee, which meant that Joe was already up and getting ready for work. I pushed feet into slippers and followed the coffee smells into the kitchen.

"Good morning," Joe said quietly. "Listen . . . hear that? I think the cats have a mouse cornered in the living room."

I listened. Squeaking and clicking noises. I yawned, wondering why we had such vocal mice. After shuffling around the kitchen for a while in a fog, I decided I needed a little more sleep. I told Joe so and headed back down the hall to the bedroom.

Snuggled down under the covers, I could hear the noises from the living room very clearly. It seemed they were getting louder, and I had never heard such odd mouse sounds. I lay on my side, facing the open bedroom door, and was surprised to see Kit Kat march by the bedroom en route to the kitchen. Which meant she'd left the living room. Which was unusual. Why would Kit Kat the Killer leave Lucy alone with a hunt in progress?

The noises of the victim grew louder and closer. It occurred to me that Lucy might chase her prey into the bedroom, and that would not be good. I stood up to close the bedroom door, and my eye caught Lucy's shadow leaping in the dark in the hallway. *What a weird little cat*, I thought.

I turned on the hall light and was astonished to find Lucy standing over a bat spread-eagled on the hall carpet at the foot of the stairs. She had nailed it right out of the air. Lucy looked thrilled over the capture of this creature that might have seemed to her to be both mouse and bird. This was even better than the mouse from the sky in the mudroom.

I, however, was horrified. The thing was almost as big as Lucy.

"Joseph!" I hissed. *"Joseph!"*

Joe appeared in the kitchen door. "What?"

"Lucy has a bat!"

He hurried over to the foot of the stairs and stared.

"Get it out of here!" I whined.

Joe grabbed the first thing he saw that made sense to him—a vintage, embroidered pillowcase I had hand-washed and line-dried just the day before. He threw it over the bat.

"Not *that*!"

"Then get me something else!" he barked.

I flew into the kitchen and, remembering Mr. Volunteer Fireman's strategy with the owl, grabbed our twin Tazmanian Devil oven mitts. I ran back to Joe.

The oven mitts were perfect, and I would certainly recommend them for such situations. Joe slipped them on and picked up the bat, much to Lucy's dismay. He squatted down for a minute to show the bat to Lucy, and we praised her and stroked her while she preened. Then I opened the front door so Joe could step out.

He took the stunned bat into the front yard, where he set it in the grass and stepped back. The bat had apparently been playing dead with Lucy. Now it shuddered. Then it spread its wings, took a few steps, and hurled itself up and into the morning dark.

Joe came inside and looked at one very pleased Lucy. "That's it," he announced. "We've got to find where the bats are coming in."

Frank the handyman dropped by that week. He reported that our walls could not be insulated, as they were three bricks deep without any space between them, which it turned out was the local method of building brick houses in 1842. He also reported that there was no insulation in the attic. There were, however, several bats living there, hanging upside down. There were also two large pyramids of dead bats and bat guano. Or bat "doings," as my mother might say. No wonder the house stank sometimes and I could not figure out why.

Frank went on. "I see where they're coming in under the overhang at that southwest bedroom. I can seal that up. And I'll clean up the attic floor before I blow the insulation in."

"What about the bats that are living up there?" I asked.

"Oh, I'll get 'em with a baseball bat," Frank said.

Joe and I glanced at each other but said nothing right then. We didn't want to kill the bats. We just wanted to evict the bats and keep them from coming back inside.

It was Russell, our termite man, who filled us in on the world of bats. Of course here in farm country, everyone praises bats for eating mosquitoes even though, in this writer's opinion, they do a mighty poor job of it. We had a nice 10' x 20' patio filled with wicker furniture every summer, but we couldn't sit outside from mid-June through mid-September because of mosquitoes. So while Joe and I didn't consider our bats to be working pets, we nevertheless didn't want to kill anything.

We asked Russell for advice, and he promptly warned us, "Don't kill them. They're protected by law."

We had no idea.

"Bats live in about three different residences," he continued. "They clean out the insects in one, then move on and do the same in the next place, then move on and do the same in the next place, then repeat the cycle." I thought of my folks, moving from the farmhouse to the lake house to the place in Florida, all in a year's time.

"Chances are," Russell continued, "when you're ready to seal up the spot where they're coming inside, they won't even be here. If they are, call me. I'll set a flea bomb up there and get them to move on. Then you can seal it up."

Russell was right. When Frank came back to do his work, the bats had moved on to the lake house or wherever our particular bats liked to go. Frank and his sons sealed up the outside, cleaned out the attic, and blew in twelve inches of insulation. Between the insulation and new windows, we stayed nice and toasty every winter after.

If cats have hopes, I suspect Lucy hoped another one of those mice with wings might some day, some way, come inside and play with her. But fortunately, we never saw another bat in the house.

·13·

My Catalyst

A dog will sit beside you while you work.
A cat will sit on the work.

Pam Brown

A few years after we landed in Michigan, I was checking out at the grocery store on Mother's Day. The clerk beamed at me and said, "Happy Mother's Day!"

"Happy Mother's Day to you too," I responded.

She continued. "Got kids?"

"No, no children."

She looked horrified. "None?"

I shook my head.

Then she said in what seemed like a worried tone, "Grand-kids?"

Hmm. I pat myself on the back that I did *not* say, "Not yet." Instead, I said, "No. But I do have cats."

She beamed again. "Oh, then *they're* your babies."

She was right about that.

I have never had children. I like children and love babies, but this was not to be. I lived many years for my career, and that kept me moving around geographically. It kept me unsettled in terms of my home life, though not unhappily so. By the time Joe and I met and married, we agreed it was too late to have children. That was okay, though I must say that once my friends started becoming grandparents, I began feeling some envy.

So I have not had the experience of holding my own baby in my arms and rocking it to sleep. I have held and rocked other people's babies and enjoyed that, and I remember once holding my toddler niece after her bath, inhaling her clean smell and feeling the strongest urge to nibble on the back of her neck with its damp curls. But except for one oddly hormonal year in my early thirties when I lived in New York City and literally craved to hold every baby I saw on the street, I was never inclined to want to get pregnant nor was I upset about not having children. Whatever maternal instincts lived within me lived quietly.

Then Kit Kat walked into our lives and unleashed a passionate urge in me to mother her. Was it because of her diagnosis of a terminal illness? Was it a distraction from dealing with the death of my birth mother? Perhaps it was because Kit Kat was a little orphan who was tough on the outside and a marshmallow inside, something that resonated with me.

Even after the maternal thing calmed down from a near scream to a murmur, I continued to rock Kit Kat when she needed nurturing, and that nurtured me in return. Having fended for herself in the wild, Kit Kat was not inclined to keep her claws in. When I rocked her and she purred and flexed her toes, she would also lightly sink those claws into me. That was okay. As my friend Jeanette once told me, "A purring cat can do whatever it wants with me." I agreed. I rocked my purring cat and gently extracted her claws from me when they got too intense.

With the appearance of Lucy, I had another little cat to hold and rock. The bonus was that this one never put her claws into me. She flexed them in the air a bit, and she liked to crawl on my shoulder sometimes and chew on my hair until she got more mature. But she kept her claws in. Eventually the day would come when she would push her paws against me like Kit Kat in that gesture to release cat-momma's milk, but still Lucy kept her claws sheathed. I eventually read that it is typical of the Russian Blue to keep their claws in during interaction with their preferred humans. Indeed, I was Lucy's preferred human—her pair-bond—and she loved the very scent of me.

It was during the early days of Lucy that I read that one reason cats make such attractive house pets is their similarity to human babies. They are about the same size and heft, and they have wide eyes and small, wide-set ears on a small head, all like a human baby. In Lucy's case, she would reach up to my face and touch it with her paw. Very human-like.

To be honest, it felt good to hold Kit Kat and Lucy and to treat them in some ways as though they were my babies. It fed something inside me, and I was highly conscious of it.

But while it felt good, it also felt a little weird. These were, after all, animals, and there was no getting around that.

During this time, I began writing and selling animal stories. This also felt good but uncomfortable—in a literary sense, that is. Let me explain.

I am a poet. The decade I lived in San Francisco, I achieved some status as a poet—enough so that when Joe and I decided to move to Michigan, one San Francisco poet completely chewed me out about it. "It takes years," she said, "to achieve the kind of respect as a poet you've achieved in this city. And you're throwing it all away."

I reminded her that I needed to be closer to my aging parents.

"Parents get old and die all the time," she barked back. "You can never get this kind of prestige again."

I chose to take her response as a compliment.

But moving to rural Michigan was tough on me after ten years of urban, artsy life in the North Beach neighborhood of San Francisco. For one thing, it meant something to be a poet in the Bay Area. There were poetry events somewhere every day and every night, and I was invited to read my work at libraries, bookstores, art galleries, benefits, street fairs, even, of all things, a longshoreman's bar full of dock workers. Small presses approached me to publish my poems. I had the privilege of studying under internationally famous and respected poets. I won some prizes. I helped run workshops and readings and served on the board of a nonprofit writers' organization in San Francisco.

In addition to living in a rich poetry community, I found that writer's block was never a problem for me in that foggy city; I seemed to be a walking bundle of productivity. Everyday events acted as catalysts for creativity. In particular, I spent hours writing in my notebooks while hanging out in North Beach's crowded Italian coffeehouses where the juke-boxes played opera and old Italian men sang along.

Now I was trying to find creative stimulation back in the land I had chosen to leave many years ago. This wasn't easy. There was a huge disconnect in every way, from the relative meaninglessness of being a poet in my hometown to the sudden, nasty appearance of writer's block in my life.

I tended to get ideas and writing energy from being around people, but writing in local joints in the Moscow area meant sitting with smokers. And in those days people smoked with a vengeance. The first time I took Joe home to meet extended family and friends, he remarked later, "Even the cats and dogs smoke in Michigan."

So I did my writing at home. But in the early days of the farmhouse, I simply could not write poems. Who knows why. When Kit Kat came to us, I found myself writing the story of her journey back to us, and I enjoyed writing it. I sold that story. During Kit Kat's first few months with us, Alberta the banty hen strayed into our yard. I wrote about that and sold the story. I wrote about my parents' dog, the horses I grew up with, my brother-in-law's longhorns, my friend's dairy cows, the wild parrots of San Francisco—and I sold every story. Then I was contracted to collect stories for anthologies—one about cats, one about dogs. More income from animal writing.

What was happening? Frankly, I felt I'd lost my mind in a couple of ways. For one thing, I was rocking cat babies, for crying out loud. And I was no longer writing anything that was, as they say, "literary." I mean, certainly I believe they were well-crafted narratives—the editors who bought them must have thought so anyway—but they were not pieces of writing I'd be able to use to get a literary grant or an MFA.

It wasn't simply because I was writing aw-shucks animal stories. Out there on the plain that first year, in an area remote enough that we couldn't get a pizza delivered, I found myself unable to write a poem for the longest time. Eventually I forced myself to gather my skills of observation and write about what was actually around me, whether I wanted to or not. I told myself to pretend I was in Siberia and to write about what I saw.

My grown nephews came over to do some heavy lifting one morning. They stood in the yard, and the older one waved his hand toward the west field, which was fallow and overgrown. "You know," he said matter-of-factly, "there are probably deer sleeping in that field right now as we speak." The younger one nodded.

This knocked me out. My nephews were country boys who knew the ways of nature well, and the thought that deer would be sleeping so close without my seeing them was fascinating.

The next day, I had business in a town a hundred miles away, and I drove the whole distance on two-lane country roads. That day, I saw huge red barns and empty deer blinds in fields of melting snow. Peacocks dragging their tails in the snow. Horses sitting right down in the snow. All kinds of what were suddenly wonderful, vibrant things to see.

When I returned home, I started a poem that was jam-packed with animals. I included the horses and the peacocks, and also the sleeping deer and my sister's pregnant heifers. I even threw in the coyote I'd heard at night but had never seen. In spite of this cast of thousands from the animal world,

I ended up with a decent poem about a snowy first day of spring, and I liked the poem, which I was later to sell twice. The result was that I was able to write poems again—not as many as I had been writing in San Francisco, but at least I was writing them.

At the same time, I realized something once again: I had deeply missed having animals in my life during those two decades of moving around. I felt very much at home in city life, but my experience in cities was one without animals. That strong childhood connection to animals had been on hiatus. Now I found that being around them, interacting with them, thinking about them, and, yes, writing about them was very grounding for me.

Fast forward three years to a hot, hot day in August. Home alone in the farmhouse, I walked by the kitchen window at 1:00 in the afternoon, and there in the side yard, oblivious to the noises of daytime around him and apparently unafraid, a coyote rolled in the grass. Right in the yard next to the driveway. I had to identify this creature through process of elimination because I'd never actually seen a coyote in daylight. His coppery coat gleamed in the sun as he rolled on his back. He stood and strolled around, sniffing things. He rolled in the grass again. For a full thirty minutes, I watched him frolic.

During the entire time, a butterfly flew up and down in front of the window, up and down, its vertical fluttering directly in my line of vision while I watched the coyote. For me, this was nothing short of magical. At one point I slipped out the back door and took a picture of the coyote, who never saw me. Unfortunately, I later discovered the camera had no film.

After several days, it occurred to me that the coyote had in essence acted out the last stanza of that earlier poem, wherein my poem-coyote has feelings he doesn't usually have because of a drastic change in weather. In the poem, it's a snowy first day of spring, the last line reading: "On this day, he does not wish to smell the fear of any living thing." In real life, the drastic change in weather was a boiling hot day, and there was Mr. Coyote, doing things I'd never known coyotes to do in my yard in daylight, clearly fearless. My poem had come full circle.

This had an odd and strong impact on me, because although the dry spell of writing poetry had been broken years before, I still didn't like where Joe and I were planted. I missed San Francisco. But after the day of the coyote, I began to relax about where I was. It was then that my writing life exploded right there in rural Michigan. I continued to write new poems and to get them published. I was asked to give seminars and readings and was paid for them. My poetry was nominated for a Pushcart Prize, the jewel of the small presses. I was solicited to write a book about haiku, the Japanese poetry form, and also several books for young readers. Things grew better for me.

During this time, Lucy and I started a new ritual on weekends. Kit Kat insisted I rise at the usual weekday time of 5:00 or 5:30 by plopping her fifteen pounds on top of me, invariably landing in the vicinity of my bladder. Or by gently biting my feet—and heaven help us during time changes. While Joe slept in, I would get out of bed, feed the cats, and make coffee. After a short session of grooming, Kit Kat strolled back to bed where she took my place next to Joe, even placing her head on my pillow, the little vixen. Lucy, on the other hand, would romp from window to window, her video screens to the world even in pre-dawn darkness.

In those days, I moved furniture around in the living and dining rooms until I found something that worked for me. The *feng shui* design people have theories about this, of course. All I know is that I started curling up in a wingback chair in a corner those mornings to drink my coffee and write in my journal, and it finally felt right. After a while, when Kit Kat headed back to bed, Lucy began crawling onto my lap for cuddling. She would fall asleep as I held her and rocked her. Since I could not write with my arms full of Lucy, I would watch daylight approach through the long windows and let my mind wander.

One day I concentrated on those windows. I could see five of them in my line of vision from the corner chair, plus what old-timers called the undertaker's door—a door with windowpanes that opened from the dining room directly to the outdoors. I liked it that the windows and door were original cuts in the brick. I wondered, not for the first time, who built this house. What were they like, those generations of people who lived here before me? What did they see out those same windows? When were those maple trees, which now stood four stories high, planted?

As I rocked and held the sleeping Lucy on these weekend mornings and let my imagination travel to where it wished, images came to me. In my mind's eye, I saw a woman living in my house after the Civil War. I never found a name for her, but I knew her. No, she was not I. And she was not a ghost. But her life—lived in my own house—played out in my mind's eye as I held Lucy.

I began keeping a separate notebook next to the chair, and when Lucy awakened and scampered off to play, I wrote furiously, filling pages with images that fell out of me with unusual ease. I had found some kind of catalyst, and it seemed to kick in because of my relaxation while holding Lucy. I continued scribbling down images and turning them into poems, faster than I'd ever written poems. These turned into a series. That turned into a full collection. Most of the poems in that collection were published individually, and down the road, I would begin performing them as a collection, accompanied by a talented violist named Clyde.

At the same time, I continued my writing about animals. I seemed unable to help myself. I just enjoyed it so much. I wrote in the dark early hours about my beasts who were always nearby. They loved to hang out in the mudroom with me, climbing all over their window condo and enjoying the stacks of books and piles of paper the way cats do.

I became shameless about asking other writers about their cats, a favored companion of people who live by the pen. Once when I taught a small workshop of adult poets in Oregon, I asked how many of them had cats. All fourteen of them shot their hands in the air. And beamed.

During these years in the Moscow house, I became employed part-time by a publishing house a few counties away. I drove to their offices a few days per month for meetings. This included brainstorming about book covers. One day the art director, an extreme cat-lover named Cheryl, brought a cover concept for a new book to me. She dropped it on my desk. "What do you think?" she said.

I looked at it. It was nice, but it seemed to be missing something, and I told her so.

Cheryl shrugged and said matter-of-factly, "I think any cover can be enhanced by putting a cat on it."

I looked at Cheryl. Cheryl looked at me. Something clicked

between us, and we smiled at each other with the thrill of co-conspirators everywhere and for all time. A new cover was born. With a cat. It filled out the cover perfectly. From then on, sometimes Cheryl and I looked at a cover that wasn't working, and our battle cry became a running joke: "Put a cat on it." But on occasion, Cheryl *did* put a cat on it.

In the meantime, I continued writing about animals. Once I decided to indulge myself in this newfound pleasure, there was no turning back.

Better yet, I continued to indulge my other secret pleasure— that of rocking my cat babies. I promised myself that for the rest of my life, I would always rock cat babies, even when these beloved ones were gone. For now, anytime Kit Kat or Lucy wanted some mothering, I would be there.

And I did not allow myself to feel silly about it. Not one bit.

·14·

ANXIETIES OLD
AND NEW

Cats seem to go on the principle that
it never hurts to ask for what you want.

Joseph Wood Krutch

With this new feline duo in my life, my general sense of joy
was much improved. How could it not be? I was no longer
alone all day while Joe worked in another town. Now I lived
my days alongside sweet and intelligent beasts. They made
such a difference for me, especially when anxiety flared.

I am an introvert who often presents as an extrovert. People
who know me probably describe me as down-to-earth, outgo-
ing, and funny. Am I presenting a false self? No. I was trained
from an early age to keep what's going on inside to myself.

Despite having chronic anxiety from childhood, I have

managed to live a full and relatively happy life. I'm lucky that way. My bucket list is not all that long now, and I've been blessed to live in exciting places, to make a living doing what I like to do, and to love and be loved. The sweetest surprise in my middle age became my husband, an extraordinary man. I've wound up living the life I had always hoped to live.

Depression has at times put me down temporarily, but I've crawled out of that more than once, mostly with professional help. I'm lucky that way too—and very grateful for my health insurance throughout the years, because talk therapy has worked wonders for me. I don't medicate for anxiety or depression and never have, though that option is there should I need it.

It has been a process for me to understand how my mind works and how to work with it. In childhood, normal happenings could take on a dark tone for no reason that I could see, and I'd have to ride it out until the dark feelings went away. In addition, I developed a kind of dissociation in childhood—a separation or disconnection from reality—that was frightening. I was in dread of these dissociative episodes hitting me and afraid while they lasted—adrenaline-pumping afraid. Fortunately such episodes were brief.

The specific kind of dissociation that troubled me is called *derealization*. This was where everything around me took on a sense of unreality that was impossible to understand and scary for a worried child to experience. It happened maybe once a week, was always a surprise, and when it presented itself, I felt quite alone. When an episode hit, I could not voluntarily pull out of it. I simply had to wait until it was over. I would pray desperately to be let out of the episode.

But even God seemed far away at such times, which made the event much scarier for a praying child.

Other people around me didn't seem to experience these episodes, and I didn't have the language to describe what was happening inside me. I'm not sure I have the right language even today. Mayo Clinic's website describes derealization as when the world "seems unreal." Well, sure, but it was far worse than that—rather, the outside world became so unhinged that it didn't seem to exist. I was there, but the world was moving away from me, leaving me afraid and questioning: *Is anything around me real? What if, this time, this feeling never goes away?*

The first time I saw a movie that showed someone in outer space accidentally floating away from safety into the weight-less black, I was terrified. Such images became a phobic issue for me, and for years, I couldn't watch any movies that took place in space. I realize now it was because that's how de-realization felt to me—never-ending isolation and darkness no matter what was around me, no beginning, no end, no control—and seemingly no tether. Fortunately, such episodes were short, and today, I almost never experience them—maybe once every several years. Now I know how to handle it if one hits. These days, I experience more general anxiety with an occasional spike.

People who know me well are aware of my anxiety disorder because I began talking about it a few years ago. But I'm not sure they'd know about it otherwise. From an early age I'd found ways not to show my fears, and as I grew older, I was encouraged to keep difficult feelings to myself. Some of that was the old-school stoicism of my Midwestern family, telling me things like, "Depressed? Well, *I* don't have time to be depressed—why do you?" I truly think they thought denial was the best way to cope.

With good therapists, I learned techniques to pull out of anxiety. My current therapist has taught me how to understand why I'm feeling my feelings and how to breathe to let go of fear. I recently started my own kind of focused prayer and meditation specifically for my anxiety, and it helps. Thinking of a particular piece of music can usually dissolve obsessive thoughts from looping in my head. Oxygen-producing exercise is very important. So is laughter.

And—no surprise here—so are animals. I was leaning on them for stability from an early age. Stroking my cats or scratching the top of my dog's head. Petting the soft noses of our gentle ponies and running my fingers through their coarse manes. As I've aged, watching any living creature works—fish swimming in a tank, birds interacting on the deck, deer drinking at the pond, and of course my family's longhorns moving about in the field. But it's especially cats for me.

A few years ago I attended a conference in Nashville, and after a couple of days, I began to have chills and a sudden sore throat. I could tell I was running a fever. I also had a lapse in logic because at six in the evening, I decided I had to go home. Now. I told the events people that I needed to leave, and I—who rarely drives any distance in the dark after 8:00 p.m. because driving in the dark makes me sleepy—got in my car to begin the all-night, eight-hour drive to southern Michigan. What was I thinking?

I remember driving through Kentucky cave country with a screaming fever that had me feeling like my scalp was being tugged off my head. I kicked myself for not staying overnight in Nashville, but the journey was rolling, so I had to roll with it. In the middle of Indiana I knew I had to lie down. I found a chain hotel where I could use frequent-guest points. It had one available room on this busy Saturday night, and that room reeked of cigarettes. I opened the window to get some air, only to see there was no screen. Who doesn't have a screen on a window in Indiana? I left it open, slept like the dead for four hours, then hit the road again.

When I arrived home exhausted and still feverish, I walked into the house, kicked off my shoes, and crawled into bed with all my clothes on. Immediately, Kit Kat and Lucy appeared. They hopped on the bed, sniffed and looked me over, then each took a position flanking me, and hunkered down. I went right to sleep.

Joe left for the store to buy Tylenol for me. When he returned, the girls turned their placid faces to acknowledge him, but they did not leave me. They kept at their posts all day and into the next. Of course I needed my human to get me pills and a glass of water. But my cats offered their kind of support— tucking in for the distance and keeping an eye on me. That is part of the human-animal bond that makes such a difference.

A few years ago in Ann Arbor, I heard writer Meg Daley Olmert, author of *Made for Each Other*, speak about research on that human-animal bond. What I remember most was this—that before the Industrial Revolution, humans and animals were constantly in each other's lives. We had symbiotic relationships in which humans and animals lived and worked together for transportation, livelihood, food. Because of this, we humans spent much of our time doing what Olmert called "watching the animals." They mattered in our daily lives, literally impacting our survival.

After the Industrial Revolution, only some of us in Western civilizations still "watch" animals. There is no longer the practical need to have animals in our lives, and many people don't interact with them at all anymore. But there are other benefits to being with animals, Olmert told the audience, and I'm paraphrasing what she said: *Is it any wonder that in the twentieth century, once we stopped watching the animals, we saw such a rise in psychotropic drug use?*

I remember sitting in the audience and absorbing this theory. It made perfect sense to me. I felt fortunate that, even though by the time I was born my family no longer depended on animals for anything, animals were always around. We always had pets. Our property was surrounded by animals—domestic and wild.

For spending money, my sister and I worked in the neighboring farmer's strawberry fields. Planting strawberries meant riding in a wagon next to a mechanical Ferris wheel–like contraption and placing a plant in it every few seconds. As the wheel slowly turned, the captured plants were slipped into the soil one at a time. It was a monotonous, repetitious job, the kind you dream about all night after a workday.

But the cool thing to me then and now was that this farmer still used a team of two draft horses in the field instead of a tractor. He sat on the front of the wagon with his long leather reins and spoke to those magnificent animals. Those gorgeous horses helped me get through a hot day. I think it's rare for an American baby boomer to have had working experience behind horses. To this day, I pay my entrance fee at our county fair just to go to the barns and see the giant, handsome Percherons.

So I grew up "watching" animals. And so did my sister.

The longhorn ranchers in her circle marvel that she can tell them when their females are in heat before it's apparent to the owners. How does my sister know? She can't tell me. She just knows. She "watches" and understands.

These many years later, while Joe and I watched the animals in our Moscow house, such attention was reciprocated. Kit Kat and Lucy were certainly watching us. Kit Kat always observed us for stress she could help alleviate. But we learned Lucy was watching too—and listening—not simply as an also-ran, but for different reasons. Kit Kat was The Comforter. Lucy turned out to be The Peacemaker.

It started one day when Joe and I got into a shouting match about something. Yes, we fight. We both have expressive, strong personalities. We love and enjoy one another, but we're both verbal, and we'd unfortunately allowed ourselves to raise our voices more frequently than we should. No kids, no neighbors, why not? On such occasions, the cats usually would simply leave the room in apparent disgust.

This day, Joe and I were mighty angry at one another. I believe it was about money, since most of our fights back then were about money. And we were both *right*. Ask either of us. We followed each other from room to room, making our points. Finally, in the kitchen, the accusations grew louder. We stood about four feet apart volleying our stupid remarks . . . until we heard a steady staccato of meows. Loud meows.

We both stopped talking and looked at the floor. Lucy, our shy blue cat, marched back and forth between us, vocalizing—*MeOW, meOW, meOW* . . . She was loud enough that we could hear her over our own raised voices. Back and forth, back and forth she stalked, meowing in a rhythm as if to say, "Stop it, stop it, *stop* it!"

Joe and I looked at each other. "Is this because of us?" he said.

"I think so."

We suddenly felt embarrassed. Our gentle blue cat had to stop us from fighting. Literally. We both began to smile. Joe reached over and wrapped his arms around me and said, "Look, Lucy—it's all okay."

Lucy looked hard at each of us, gave a final squawk, and then scampered out of the room. From then on, any time voices started to rise, Lucy would run into the room and look at our faces and do that staccato meow. And we would always calm down. Eventually we rarely fought at all. That's why we gave our girl the title of Peacemaker.

Clearly our cats were taking care of us.

On the morning of September 11, 2001, I was working in Grand Rapids, Michigan, which was about a hundred country miles from our Moscow house. I was in a meeting that included off-site people on phones, and one of them said, "Do you know a plane just hit the World Trade Center in New York?"

So began that horrendous day. I became quietly frantic. As is my nature when I'm exceptionally worried, I simply wanted to be home. After I learned that both buildings collapsed, I got in my car and headed for Moscow. The hundred-mile drive was through back roads and farm towns—my Geo Metro was hard for truck drivers to see, even in their mirrors, so I stayed off the interstates. On this day, every small town had long lines at the gas stations, where gas had suddenly tripled in price. I had an almost-full tank, and yet three times I pulled into a gas line in a panic. I reasoned with myself each time to snap out of it and get back on the road.

Joe and I arrived home at the same time. We walked into the house together and at first said very little. Neither of us had seen any of the footage, so Joe finally took my hand and said, "Let's watch."

We sat on the couch and turned on the TV to images that made me weep. Even hours after the fact, my adrenaline shot up as we watched. After a while, we realized that both Kit Kat and Lucy had silently appeared and were lying on the top of the couch, one of them perched behind each of our heads. "They know something's wrong," Joe said. I had to agree.

I cannot begin to imagine being closer to the carnage—or losing loved ones there. For days, even that far from the affected areas, I felt a back-burner terror that tapped straight into my childhood fears during the JFK years. Back then, fears of missile attacks were always afoot in America. We had neighbors who, like many Americans, dug out a bomb shelter in their back yard and filled it with food and provisions. The county fair showed how to build and stock such places. I became afraid of ordinary things like noon sirens and low-flying airplanes. Then came the assassination of President Kennedy.

For the rest of 2001, I was reminded of those childhood days. I felt especially fortunate to have the calming effects of Kit Kat and Lucy at my side—intelligent animals bolstering me with their presence, eyes wide with curiosity or slanted in circumspection, checking Joe or me for stress points. Tails twitching. Waiting. Showing up where needed.

In the months following the 9/11 tragedies, Joe's job required extra work hours to meet a Homeland Security–mandated deadline. His commute was already over an hour long each way, most of it on two-lane country roads, and all in the dark for much of the year. Now he was coming home around 9:00 or 10:00 at night. Sometimes he arrived home so exhausted that he would walk in the back door, head straight through the house to the bedroom, and lie down without taking off coat or shoes. He'd fall immediately asleep.

After waiting so intently for Joe to come home, Kit Kat would follow him through the house, hop on the bed, and check him over, sniffing his shoes, his coat, his hair. Then she would lie down next to him, leaning on his legs like a herding collie might, continuing to eye him. Whenever I checked in on them, Kit Kat was awake. She would turn her face to me and meet my eyes as if to say, "I've got this." I would then leave them so Joe could rest for a while. Clearly he was in good paws.

My friend Claudia is an art therapist. While she was raising her kids, they had many pets, but never a cat. When she comes to my home, she enjoys watching our girls but probably is a dog person inside. I had not yet told her about writing this book when I received an email from her that clearly spoke to it.

Claudia had been shoring up her childhood home on Lake Erie. This task had a tremendous amount of stress attached to it, between money woes, inspectors, and sore muscles. One day, after working hard at the house, she took a breather. Here's what she wrote me by email:

> I was outside . . . A cat came around the fence. Kind of a ginger tiger. Folded ears, square head, amber eyes. It followed me back to the chair by the water, settling in the shade underneath. Next thing I know, it's jumped onto my lap nestling! Climbed up my chest to make eye contact and rub under my

chin. Licked my hands and arm then settled down to just be scratched and tickled around its head.

She ended with: *Did you send it?*

Oh Claudia . . . how I wish I had the power to send a cat where it's needed. Fortunately for me, for you, and for millions of others, cats seem to figure out where they're needed all by themselves.

·15·

TEN MILES

Way down deep, we're all motivated by
the same urges. Cats have the courage
to live by them.

Jim Davis

Although having Kit Kat and Lucy in my life turned out to
be a fine way to self-medicate anxiety, their presence could
also, like the cats of my childhood, ramp up my feelings of
worry and dread.

We kept Kit Kat and Lucy indoors 24/7. That contrib-
uted to their safety, and having this much control over my
pets' well-being helped me. Other than an occasional stress-
provoked nightmare that Lucy would somehow get out of
the house (I mostly feared Lucy getting outside), things were
fairly anxiety-free regarding my cats' welfare.

Unless, that is, someone got sick. When a cat was ill, I was on high alert. I don't recall a sick cat ever getting well when I was growing up—they seldom were taken to the vet, so it was a special fear for me as an adult to have a sick cat. When they seemed under the weather, I watched them carefully, as I knew cats can go down pretty quickly.

Then one day, Kit Kat became very ill—vomiting, lethargic, feverish.

Cat people know that cats vomit. It's a part of living with some cats, and once you know your own cat, you know whether the vomiting or the frequency of it should be a concern or not. For Kit Kat, I could see this vomiting was a concern, and I took her to our new vet clinic ten miles away.

When Kit Kat didn't respond as quickly to treatment as a cat her young age should, they decided to test her for feline leukemia (FLV) and for feline infectious virus (FIV). I think that's standard testing today for all cats, but maybe not so much then. These tests were done in the office, and Kit Kat and I waited for results in an examining room. I held her close to my chest and rocked her. She was in her usual vet clinic shutdown mode, and I was on edge.

The vet walked in and dropped his file on the counter. "Well, she's negative for FLV, and that's good. But she tests positive for FIV." He looked down for a moment and allowed that information to sink in.

I scratched Kit Kat's cheeks. She stayed still. "What does that mean for her?"

"It means we need to watch for infections and hit them early with antibiotics."

I had just read an article in *Cat Fancy* about a new FIV vaccine for cats. Yes, the vet said he had the vaccine, though

Kit Kat wouldn't need it now. "If Kit Kat can remain asymptomatic, she has a good chance at a long life. Try to keep her as stress-free as you can, and we'll be on the alert when she's not feeling well."

I started breathing easier, especially when we talked about how, although they are not the same diseases, FIV closely parallels HIV in humans. Joe and I had lived in San Francisco during the years when effective drugs were finally available for people with HIV—drugs that were lengthening life and improving quality of life. In the eighties, those people would have died quickly of full-blown AIDS. But in the nineties, people were living with HIV that miraculously was not turning into actual AIDS, and they were doing well—not getting ill, able to work.

"So should we view this the same way we view people who are living with HIV and doing okay?" I asked.

The doctor nodded vigorously. "Absolutely."

Then my panic returned. "What about Lucy? Is she infected?"

"Bring her back here when you take Kit Kat home, and we'll test her." He fiddled with his folder for a minute. "You know, Kit Kat probably was born with FIV. I'd guess she acquired it from her mother. Since this disease is spread between cats much like HIV is spread between humans, it's not likely two female house cats are engaging in any behavior that would infect one another. But let's see. If Lucy's negative, we'll vaccinate her."

I packed Kit Kat up and drove the ten miles home, crying all the way. I rushed Lucy back and waited with her in the examining room for test results that turned out to be good news. She tested negative for both FLV and FIV. I cried all the way home again—this time with relief.

When Joe arrived home from work, I placed Kit Kat on the bed and had Joe join us. I told him the news. He took it all in quietly. For a while we both petted Kit Kat in silence. Then Joe spoke. He reminded me of the people we had known in San Francisco—residents in our apartment building, co-workers, my hairdresser in North Beach—all who were living full lives with HIV. He further reminded me that our cat was a tough little beast. With our assistance, he believed she could do fine living with FIV. So we made a pact not to worry about this unless she became ill.

I was relieved that Lucy had not acquired the virus. In general, her health had been good right from the start. She came to us with a case of worms, which caused that five-pound kitten to pass gas so horrendous she could clear a room. As one can imagine, we handled that quickly. She also had hairball tendencies. But that was it.

Kit Kat needed more attention. And she was not through with infections. We had another worrisome hospitalization, and fortunately, she pulled through again. That time, however, when I picked her up, the staff showed me that they'd left a port in her front right leg in case she needed to return. They had bandaged it snugly so Kit Kat couldn't expose it.

But I knew my OCD cat better than they did. "You do know," I said, "that she's going to get that bandage off."

"No, she won't be able to."

Sigh.

I drove Kit Kat home with her bandaged leg. Once there, of course Kit Kat the Obsessive paid no attention whatsoever to her familiar surroundings. She ignored her sister and she ignored me. She proceeded to spend every moment licking

the bandage. I could hear that rough cat tongue working—
scrape, scrape . . .

Kit Kat was so in the zone during this day of licking the
bandage that she even ignored her food—and as I've noted,
this cat was highly food-driven. So on this day back home from
hospitalization, it was odd indeed that, even though Kit Kat
hadn't eaten much for several days, food was not on her agenda.
Our cat had one thing and one thing only in mind: getting that
bandage off her leg. She licked and licked and licked until,
after several hours, she succeeded in exposing part of the port.

I called the clinic. At first they couldn't believe it, and
I am pleased to report that I refrained from saying, "Told
you so . . ."

"Well then, bring her in," they said, "and we'll remove it."

I drove the ten miles back to the vet. They removed the
port. I think I heard a big feline sigh of relief as Kit Kat and
I got back in the car.

Once we returned home, dinner was served, and a happy
cat sat down and ate.

Joe and I would accommodate our OCD Kit Kat to the best
of our ability. But after her FIV diagnosis, we were especially
determined not to stress our girl any more than necessary.
Like my childhood OCD dog Buster, Kit Kat was worth the
extra attention.

During the height of my concern about Kit Kat's health,
I called my friend Kathy, a fellow worrier, and I told her
about the scary new diagnosis. To my surprise, Kathy actually laughed. "Oh Lonnie," she said, "Kit Kat's not going
anywhere. Don't you know that? She has no intention of
leaving Joe and you."

Of course. Joe and I knew without a doubt that this strong-willed cat would do whatever she must to be with us. She had already proven it with her dangerous journey back to us from the longhorn ranch. And now she was not letting FIV keep her down. The powerful Kit Kat would continue to insist that her circumstances go the way she wanted them to go, and we mere humans obliged her. She was determined and full of heart. And she wanted to live. With us.

In the years that followed, regardless of FIV and any subsequent infections, Kit Kat would live far more than her allotted nine lives.

·16·

THAT YEAR

Our perfect companions never have
fewer than four feet.

Colette

Five years into living in the Moscow house, I woke up on
Christmas Day to a heavy snowfall. It had been green most
of December, so this morning I felt instantly happy for every
kid in the county. Then I felt happy for *me*, waking up in
our big, chilly old house with Joe next to me and our two
sleeping cats curled around us. I snuggled under the down
comforter for a little longer.

Slowly it occurred to me that I'd had a dream in which
Kit Kat and Lucy could speak. I tried to recall the details but
couldn't. I remembered a myth that all the barnyard animals
speak on Christmas Eve. For a while that Christmas morning,

I stayed under the covers, wondering what our girls would say if they could speak.

Or did speak . . . ?

I smiled to myself, got up, and left Joe sleeping. There would be several of us celebrating the holiday at our house, so I had some preparations to do. As I headed for the coffeemaker, Kit Kat and Lucy followed me down the hall for their morning feeding. They split a small can of holiday cat food. Then Kit Kat, per usual, sailed back to bed for more Joe Time while Lucy sat down on a kitchen chair and washed her face with her paws. I knew she would stay with me in the kitchen.

While Kit Kat tended to eat and run, Lucy enjoyed observing kitchen work. She liked to sit on a chair close to the table and watch me pare vegetables. She enjoyed diving after the occasional grape tomato I would toss on the floor for her and then cuffing it around with the finesse of a soccer player. Pelé had nothing on Lucy. I used to noodle on writing a series of children's books about her, the first being called *Lucy and the Grape Tomato*, wherein Lucy would bat the tomato around, follow it, and find herself in all kinds of adventures. I've not gotten very far with that. All I can say is that when we bought a new refrigerator and moved out the old one, I found where Lucy's grape tomatoes went to die.

I have always preferred Kit Kat and Lucy not get on the stove or counters or kitchen table or any area where there is food preparation. I know some cat owners feel otherwise, and it's even sometimes recommended that cats be fed on high counters, especially if there's a dog in the house. But I'd never liked it. When our cats jumped on food prep surfaces, Joe and I simply picked them up and gently set them on a chair or back down on the floor. And they usually cooperated, though who knows what kind of kitchen romping went on in our absences.

But this Christmas morning was not a typical one for me. We were in the throes of some serious life issues. I did not yet know that it would be our last Christmas in the big house, and I did not yet know that Joe and I were about to embark on our toughest year so far.

What I did know was that my mom had a terminal cancer diagnosis that she had been fighting valiantly. So far, she had added an extra year of quality living to the six-months-left-to-live prediction from her doctor. This fall, she decided to stay up north for treatment through the early part of winter, then go to her Florida home in early spring. Mom was only now starting to show the wear and tear of the cancer, and nobody was certain the next round of chemo would help. So I was glad she would be with us at the Moscow house on Christmas.

Also on my mind this day was that Kit Kat had been sick most of November, though she'd recovered by December. But it had been worrisome for a while. I had a high-maintenance author in my editorial job, and this required too much airline travel. I'm actually afraid to fly, but I do it frequently for my work. If my anxiety is especially high, I have the sensation that the plane is plummeting for the entire flight. And that is no way to fly. Unfortunately, that sensation had come back on my last flight.

So this Christmas morning, with snow lighting up the kitchen, I set about the quiet task of preparing food before reality hit too hard. I brought the washed vegetables to the table, sat down, and began to organize.

Lucy's emerald eyes grew round, smelling these things from the earth and hearing the water used to wash them. But today, on this holiday at the end of those difficult months, I wanted my gentle cat even closer to me, and I did not have time to cuddle. So I broke my own rule. I spread a bath towel on the table, picked up Lucy, and planted her on the towel. Surprised and happy, she sprawled on her side, relishing the rough texture of that line-dried terrycloth. Then she watched me pare and slice. I stopped now and then to scratch her soft fur.

As Lucy's quiet companionship helped me keep moving on this morning—a *cat-like* morning—I acknowledged that for now, everyone in my family was alive and functioning. Joe and I were relatively healthy, and we had jobs and a roof over our heads and cars that ran without fuss. Our Kit Kat was doing better, and Lucy had not been infected with Kit Kat's FIV. And Mom was still with us.

Lucy hopped down and headed for the window to watch the magic of falling snow. I thought about her arrival just before Thanksgiving a couple of years ago. She needed a home, of course, but I also believed she came to us because I needed her. In addition, Joe received another playmate to distract him from stress, and Kit Kat received one of her own species, to mother, to boss around, to cuddle, to nap with.

Once you become a grown-up, who remembers the Christmas gifts you receive? Unless it's a diamond ring or a new car, it's likely that those gifts, like so much else in our hurried-up adult world, become faded memories—or no memory at all. But for me, on the cusp of Christmas, my Lucy had appeared out of the dark and presented herself like a personal gift.

And I would need to remember such gifts—because our

last Christmas in Moscow was my mother's last Christmas in this world.

I have a lovely photo of the tree we had that year. The Fraser fir stands tall next to the arch that gently separates the living and dining rooms. The topping angel almost reaches the twelve-foot ceiling. The tree is full of ornaments I'd collected over the years, including dangling photos of Kit Kat and Lucy, gifts from Joe.

That Christmas Day, my mother spent most of her time tucked into a wingback chair in front of the tree, her slippered feet on the ottoman, an afghan over her legs. Walking in the house had been hard for her, but now that she was warm and snug right in front of the twinkling Christmas tree, her smile was constant. She adored our cats, and they took turns sitting on her lap, responding to her touch with deep purrs. They knew her well, mostly because when Joe and I traveled in summer, Mom would drive to our house and let herself in to give her grand-kittens a little extra loving while they were alone.

That last Christmas, Kit Kat stayed on Mom's lap for the longest time, constantly gazing up at her radiant face. Did my girl somehow know Mom was leaving us?

The new year rolled in and rolled on. We helped Mom with her treatment transportation, and before we knew it, she was headed to Florida. She did well while there. My mother and her people were a resilient lot, and it showed at times like these. In Florida Mom continued to entertain guests from out of state, and when I visited her in early April, she was still driving and even getting her own groceries.

But shortly after my visit, she went into the hospital, and things never improved after that. By the end of April, we flew her back to Michigan, where she moved in with my sister under hospice care.

I was with Mom for some of every day now. On her last birthday in early May, we watched from the dinner table as a longhorn gave birth in the field beyond the back yard. It seemed very life-affirming to me. But the day after Mom's birthday, she started to fade.

I had begun writing a different version of this book while Mom was living at my sister's. Writing gave me something to focus on to distract me. I was very close to my mother, always had been. The thought of her dying was a vivid childhood fear of mine that could take over my thoughts in my younger years. Now I viewed death differently—sad, but also something we live with. Still—she was my mother.

Every couple of days, I printed a new chapter to take to Mom. She would read it and comment on it and offer encouragement. We continued to do this until Mom could no longer hold the paper in her hands. Then I stopped writing and tucked everything away.

Mom wasn't afraid to die; she just didn't want to. She was a woman of faith who knew where she was going after she died, but she had no intention of going there yet. No matter what the doctors said, my mother planned to beat cancer. Although she had confidence in the next life, she really and truly did not want to leave this one, and she fought hard to stay here.

During Mom's last week, we spent lots of time together, talking. I wrote in my journal then: "It's a sad time but a soft time." Once she told me, "I sleep so well at night. Then

I wake up thinking of all the things I'm going to do, and I'm ready to jump up and do them." She seemed bewildered as she looked down at her cancer-ridden body. "And every morning I'm so surprised I can't."

I had a dream two days before Mom died. In the dream, I was standing in a cemetery next to my car. Two young men, both wearing black suits and dark glasses, approached me. I felt nervous about them, so I hurried into my car and hit the lock button. They watched the locks snap down. I cracked my window, and one of them said, "Will you tell us where you're going?" I refused and raised the window back up. I turned the car around and drove away. I watched them in the rearview mirror to see if they would follow, but they simply watched me drive away. When I woke up, I felt that I should prepare, that my mother's passing would be soon.

The following day, Mom woke up with garbled speech. As she tried to speak throughout that day, her frustration was evident. In late afternoon, she curled on her side and fell deeply asleep, so Joe and I left, emotionally drained. My sister said she'd call if anything changed.

Once home, Joe and I didn't speak much. We simply went to our bedroom and turned on the evening news, prepared to turn in early. Kit Kat and Lucy joined us on the bed. It was almost dusk.

The news blared away. I was aware of the cats running over me at some point to get to the open window on my side of the bed. I could hear a bird outside but thought nothing of it. The unruly yews under the windows had lots of bird activity, which brought plenty of viewing thrills for the cats.

Joe muted the TV and said, "Listen." The cats sat at the window, their tails slapping hard on the bedside table. There was a loud, insistent chirp coming through the screen. To my surprise one red cardinal perched on the yew branches, looking at the window screen, chirping hard.

I grew up in the country and of course knew some birds. But my mother really was more attuned to them. She taught me to watch for the first robin of spring, which after a long Michigan winter was thrilling to see. My mother kept bird feeders and wren houses, and she fed birds in the snow when she still wintered in Michigan. She often told me that she hated to see a bird in a cage. "They should be outdoors and flying, not caged up," she would say.

So I knew a little about birds, and while I didn't recognize the chirp of this bird, I certainly could recognize the scarlet brilliance of a male cardinal. He was so close and so loud that the cats were simply beside themselves.

Neither Joe nor I had any idea why this bird sat vocalizing fearlessly into our open window as dusk approached. He hopped from yew branch to the portico and back again, over and over, his chirping loud and insistent. Lucy made her signature "kill" noise—a fast clicking in the back of her mouth—but even that didn't unnerve the cardinal. Our talking didn't either.

"Do you think his mate is hurt or something?" I said.

"Let's see," Joe said. We stepped outside, and the cardinal moved to the top of the portico. He did not fly away, and he did not stop chirping. We investigated the porch and surrounding grass, even under the yews, but we saw no reason for this cardinal to be so agitated. So we went indoors.

The bird moved back to the yews and the window, and he continued chirping. He chirped so loud that when a friend called on the phone, I had to shut the window to hear her.

He chirped outside the closed window for a while longer and eventually flew away. As I fell asleep that night, it occurred to me that perhaps, like the men in the dream, the appearance of this cardinal might be some kind of message. I fell asleep trying to figure it out.

At 5:00 a.m., my sister called to say we'd better come, and Mom passed away a few minutes before we arrived. Seeing her body at rest made me realize how free from pain and frustration she was now.

My family and I sat next to Mom's bed for a time before calling hospice. Her room had an east window, and as the sun was rising, my brother-in-law remarked, "Look—a cardinal." Sure enough, a bright red cardinal swooped by the window. I briefly told my sister and brother-in-law about the chirping cardinal of the night before, but we all had other things on our minds right then.

The day lumbered on. Hospice came, the hearse came, relatives came. We made arrangements, and then Joe and I drove home. Now it was Sunday afternoon, still the same day my mother left us. Exhausted, Joe and I crawled into bed for naps. The cats joined us as the wind picked up outside. A storm was brewing in the southwest.

But I could not sleep. I began to feel panicky. I had never been in this world without my mother. I knew I was fortunate to have her with me into her old age, but my childhood fear of her dying apparently hadn't really gone away. Mom and I talked to each other almost every day of my life, and now I could never again even call her on the phone. I gave up on the nap.

I walked through the house, looked out the windows, and

cried. It slowly dawned on me that I hadn't noticed spring had come and gone. It was late May, and we were already on the cusp of summer. Those seven huge maple trees standing guard around the west and north sides of the farmhouse were fully leafed out. Now their branches and leaves moved wildly in the warm wind.

I knew there was still time before the storm would hit, so I moved to the patio where I would not disturb Joe, and I sank into a wicker chair. The sky in the west was deep gray and turbulent. The green maple leaves moving in the wind were getting noisier by the minute, and those high branches creaked. Birds had taken cover. I listened and watched and cried. It seemed that nature was expressing my feelings.

Then I heard it. Over the sound of the trees in the wind was a loud chirping. I looked up, and there in those majestic maples was one male cardinal. He swooped from tree to tree, in and out of the green branches. He was the only bird out there that I could see or hear, and he was noisy and bright red against all that green. In spite of the approaching storm, he seemed to be doing what he was born to do. It was not just that he seemed fearless; he was having an absolute blast, as if this was his own personal playground.

I watched the cardinal soar and swoop and dance around in the heavy air of this approaching storm. I listened to him chirp over the sound of the wind. For the first time in days, I felt my stomach unknot.

I believed that this was a comfort intended for me. It had been so the night before, it had been so this morning, and it was now. I felt God was bringing me peace with this audacious songbird. I felt assured right down to my toes that my mother was free of the virtual cage of aging and illness that had kept her from moving and talking. I also knew without a doubt that she was not lost to me forever, that someday I would be with her.

How long did I sit there? I'm not sure. But while I watched that flying, dancing, noisy, beautiful bird, I stopped crying.

The next morning, I rose early and went to my computer to write a eulogy for Mom's funeral. While I sat at the keyboard, I heard chirping. I looked out my mudroom window, and there on the south lawn—a lawn with no trees—a very vocal red cardinal stood in the grass. He was framed in the only window in the room. I again felt comforted and went back to my writing.

For the next couple of days, a cardinal—*the* cardinal?—hung around the house, mostly in the yews. It began to feel natural to see this little guy. I actually sat next to an open window once and watched him, and he stayed right there, perched on a yew branch, cocking his head at me, chirping. As the week went on, however, it seemed the cardinal moved farther and farther away. No longer did he sit on the yews next to the window. Sometimes I could hear him but not see him.

Then I had a vivid dream.

In the dream, my mother called on the phone from the next life. Her voice sounded young and happy, and I could hear her smile as she talked. I started crying, and I told her how much I missed her. She cooed in her motherly way. I asked her what she was trying to say to us on that last day when she could not talk, but she gently indicated that I should not ask about her time with us. That was over.

She had an almost secretive happiness, like someone who is engaged or pregnant but not yet telling anyone. In the dream she gave me a phone number to try to reach her, though she couldn't guarantee she'd be there to answer. I started to feel panic because I was losing her smiling voice. Then the connection broke. I tried the number she gave me to call her back, but it would not work. Then I woke up.

That was one week to the day since Mom had died. My friend Jeanette came over for Sunday dinner. After we ate, Joe left us alone, and Jeanette and I took our iced teas to the patio. It was a stunning day, and the birds were vocal in the maples. I decided to take the risk and tell my friend about the cardinal.

Jeanette was very moved. Then I told her my dream of the night before. When I finished, Jeanette said, "Listen . . ."

Up in the trees was the bold chirping of one cardinal, louder than all the other bird sounds. Jeanette and I looked at each other, then we tried to find him. We followed his chirp all around the seven maples in the yard, and although we both heard him loud and clear, neither of us was able to catch sight of him.

By the next day, I no longer heard him.

·17·

THE SURF SHACK

Cats don't like change without their consent.

Roger A. Caras

After Mom died, Joe and I began talking about moving away from Moscow. We felt we needed an easier house and one that was closer to civilization. This was something we had been tossing around between us for a year or so, but with Mom's cancer, we didn't have the extra energy to put such a big change as a house move into motion. And after Mom died and my sister and I began dealing with her estate in both Michigan and Florida, I was usually too fatigued to think of anything but that and my day job.

I'm not sure how long it would have taken us to get it together to actually move had Joe not totaled his car on his lengthy country-road commute. To this day I marvel that he had not yet had an accident those first six years, given the distance, the terrain, the darkness, and at times his extreme fatigue.

Joe had not grown up driving as I had. My motor-head stepdad gave me a 1965 Corvair to drive around our property when I was an unlicensed fifteen-year-old. But Joe had never driven on country roads until we moved here, had certainly never driven around herds of deer, had never even used high beams because he'd only driven in cities. Joe also had not driven in snow or on ice very much. But he immediately rose to the occasion and even in winter was an excellent country-road commuter.

In rural Michigan, everyone hits a deer at some point, but as of this writing, not Joe. I hit a deer, but Joe did not. One of my funny memories is when the two of us were traveling on a gravel road near Moscow one night, Joe at the wheel, and I could see the shadows of a herd of deer running in the dark field literally right next to us. I grabbed Joe's leg in a panic and said, "Deer . . . deer . . . deer . . ."

Joe snapped back, "What?"

My husband heard "Dear."

But now, driving through a farm town on his way to work, Joe's car was broadsided by two cars. In the process, he'd broken two fingers. He called me from the ambulance and said, "That's it. We're moving."

I loved our time at the house in Moscow. We lived there for only six years, but it seems longer, larger, like a bigger chunk of my life. I loved the handsome brick house, the glorious maples, the open sky over the fields. I loved raising the windows on nice mornings to air that was sometimes fresh, sometimes smoky, sometimes aromatic with the farm country smells of newly cut crops or manure spread over them. I enjoyed living in an area that had a thousand Amish residents—when we drove by their farms and waved, they waved back. I even liked it that we were around such whimsical businesses as Glory to God Garage (we were customers) and Sun Your Buns Tanning Salon (we were not customers).

I didn't even really mind the power outages we had so often on that plain. The first week we spent there was one of those times. Returning home one evening from an errand, we both noticed how dark the drive was down our road. It wasn't until we got to the house that we realized there was a power failure.

We got out of the car, then were both taken aback by how the sky looked. The stars were so vivid they seemed to hover very close to us. In large cities, you don't see stars at all, and until you see them again, you can forget they exist. On this night, Joe and I stared up at the stars, drop-jawed, the inconvenience of power failure momentarily gone. We held on to each other as we craned our heads in the dark so much I got dizzy.

The worst power failure would be in January one year when we had no electricity or heat for three and a half days. And this was not a mild winter. We kept the refrigerator closed with cold things inside but put frozen items in boxes in the car outside. Since we had a gas stove, we could at least boil jugs of water for instant coffee in the morning and for sink bathing. I melted snow in pasta pans, then strained the twigs and leaves out of the water so we could flush the commodes. It was weirdly fun.

On the last day of the outage, however, even Kit Kat and Lucy were getting a little ornery. Their little paw pads were like ice, so I kept them tucked into our bed as much as they could stand. When the power company workers finally showed up, I blew kisses at them from the porch. They grinned and waved.

I loved it there, yes, but it was a lot of house. It needed work that we weren't any good at. Had we been twenty years younger, we would have stayed and learned how to do the home improvements it needed. In our six years there, we put money into the house's structural and outside issues that would shore it up for future generations rather than invest in interior redos. It was the best plan, and we had good work done—new roof, soffit repair, and replacement of every window with new ones—twenty-seven double-hung windows plus five basement windows.

This was not an area where historical societies had to approve such exterior updating, and we were tired of living in drafts and watching our money go down the propane drain. So we picked out windows that looked the most compatible with the house. On a gorgeous day in September, I dragged a wicker chair into the yard and sipped coffee while watching the window people punch out every window at the same time. Seeing my home with all its windows removed was unnerving. What if they'd measured wrong?

But the workers knew what they were doing, and the new windows proved to be a good investment. They kept mice out of the basement. They sealed up the house nicely in winter—no more drafts and no more snowdrifts on the inside windowsill. In summer I learned to raise, lower, and close the windows at strategic times of the day to keep the house cooled. I'm convinced those current and workable windows sold the house to the next owners.

We had moved to that house with so few possessions. But as Joe would note, nature hates a vacuum, and we wound up acquiring so much. Too much. I furnished all those rooms with some surprisingly tasteful furniture from area yard sales. But now we needed to let go.

Of course the best part of living in the Moscow house was the arrival of Kit Kat and Lucy. I have good memories of waking up without an alarm clock at 5:00 a.m., rested and happy. I made coffee in the dark, the cats rubbing on me and talking to me. They followed me into the ugly but snug office mudroom where I spent many hours of creativity and productivity. Throughout my work time, Kit Kat and Lucy stayed nearby. They lounged in the sun on the wide window-sills, buddy-groomed each other on the loveseat next to my computer, and darted in and out of my office like friendly little sharks.

I had my family around me for a while, too, something I'd missed during my city years far away. My father had died two years before Joe and I married, but my mother, stepfather, and stepmother were all alive when we moved to Michigan. It was good to be with them in their later years and at the end of their lives. I would not have wanted to miss that. It was also a bonus to know my biological mother through her friends and family, even though I would never meet her myself.

It took time for me to shrug off what I missed about living in beautiful San Francisco. But I eventually became content with where I was. I knew it was so when I took a trip to San Francisco for business several years after we'd moved, thrilled to be back. But as I walked through my city, I heard myself thinking, *It's not mine anymore.* And while that felt sad, it also felt okay, like the right amount of time had gone by. I belonged in Michigan now.

There's one photo in particular that speaks to me of my feelings about our time in Moscow. In the picture, Joe and I sit in wicker chairs on the patio in autumn. We're ankle-deep in dry, fallen leaves. The huge west wall of the house looms behind us, and long shadows of bare maples climb up the bricks in the lowering sun. The tall windows look like so many eyes gazing off into the past. The house stands huge and solid. And that's what it was. The house was there long before we were dreamed into existence, and it will be there long after we're gone.

My friend Nancy and her husband were trying to sell an empty house on the outskirts of the town of Jackson. At lunch one day, she told me she was frustrated because the house had been on the market for a while. When I quizzed her about it, she finally said, "You want to see it?"

The area was what realtors call "exsurb"—a country road with easy access to highways and stores. The minute I saw the property, I was enchanted. The unremarkable two-bedroom ranch house with attached garage sat on a gorgeous two-to-three-acre lot. Although the house was plain, it had, as they say, good bones—it was solidly made—and that simple house was surrounded by the very best of nature.

To the east and west were woods. In the back yard was a pond, and beyond that were wetlands. Three tall and solid willow trees soared over the tree lines. A few apple trees and some maple trees were scattered around the yard, and a four-story white pine stood on the east end, so huge it provided quite a bit of shade. Later on when there was a full moon, I would see it peek between the white pine's needled branches.

The house was on the north side of Jackson, a full county away from Moscow. It was considerably smaller than where we were living. There was no basement due to the high water table in the area, which could be a worry in tornado season. On the other hand, we wouldn't be able to fill the basement with possessions like we had in Moscow.

When I first stepped inside, I saw vintage tile work in the kitchen and in the smaller bath that made me happy. I saw plenty of windows and a slider that opened to a deck, perfect for my need for natural light while working at home. Then I noticed that this small house's rooms were partly in a big circle—perfect for the cats. They had a circle of rooms in the Moscow house where they chased each other.

I told Nancy I wanted Joe to see the house and that this might be an option for us to buy. Joe noticed the exact same things about the house when he walked inside—the cheery fifties vibe and the circle of rooms. Plus the layout of rooms would work well for the way we lived, and the house was in decent shape. Joe and I looked at each other, and just as fast as we'd decided the Moscow house was for us then, we decided this little ranch house was for us now.

We took the month of September to slowly move some things in, but an actual moving day of the furniture was approaching. Joe and I had had a disagreement about how to handle the cats in this move. I thought we should be taking them back and forth to the empty house when we puttered in it so they could get used to it. Joe did not agree.

Enter again Pet Expert Donna. Turned out Joe was correct, and I should have known—he seemed to have that inside look at the cats sometimes that I didn't have.

"No," said Donna. "Do not take the cats there until moving day. That will stress them too much, and they're already wondering what you're doing with all those packing boxes. They don't want to be in a strange place where they don't have their hiding places, so only move them once."

When would I learn that cats don't think like I do?

She went on. "More pets are lost on moving days than you can imagine, so I'm going to tell you exactly what to do that will keep them safe and accounted for. If you don't want to do what I say, then board the cats for the night before and the day you move."

"I don't want to board them," I said.

"I know that, so listen to me. Pick a room in the new house and call it the Safe Room. Put a litterbox in it, and on the opposite side of the room, put their food and water. Fill it with blankets and clothes that smell like you. Take the cats over the night before the move, and leave them in the Safe Room."

I frowned. "I don't want to leave them in the house without us."

Donna shrugged. "Then board them."

I sighed. "Okay, keep going."

Donna went on. "You're going to leave the cats in their Safe Room that night. Before you leave the house, put signs all over their door instructing that it not be opened. The next day, go there with the movers, but nobody opens their door, not even you. Make sure they've got plenty of water and dry food because you're not going in their room all day.

"After the movers leave, set up your coffeepot and make

your bed. Then let the cats in your bedroom with the door closed. When you turn out the light to go to sleep, open the door. They will explore the house while you sleep, and by morning, they'll be on the bed with you. The next day, no more Safe Room—it's over."

I don't know why I was surprised that everything happened exactly as Donna suggested and predicted. We took the girls over the night before. We set up the laundry room plus the tiny bath next to it with food, water, litterbox, cat beds, and clothes that smelled like us. All set.

When I opened the doors of their carriers, however, the cats were very unhappy, worse than when they went to the vet clinic. They were hit with strange new smells, and they didn't like it one bit. Kit Kat hissed at me. She even bit me—something she only did once when she was a teenage kitten. Lucy started to walk out of her carrier, then stopped and looked around and backed back in.

But we had to do it. I cracked the window just a tad, and Joe put yellow caution tape over their door. As we walked by the window on the way to the car, we saw two little noses between the window and the sill, twitching and sniffing the air outside their new home.

The move went without a hitch. When it was over, as Donna suggested, we set up the coffeemaker and made the bed. By now, paws were sticking out of the bottom of the laundry room door, trying to get our attention. The girls were ready to leave the Safe Room.

We each picked up a cat and brought her to the bedroom and closed the door. It was fun to listen to Kit Kat vocalize as she explored the room, alternately meowing and hissing, as if to say, "Oh, I know this . . . but what's this? This is mine

. . . but whose is this?" Before Joe and I put our weary selves to bed and turned out the light, we opened the bedroom door. Every now and then, I'd wake up hearing a noise in the new house, but it sounded benign enough that I'd go back to sleep. By morning, just as Donna predicted, both Kit Kat and Lucy were on our bed, fast asleep.

The cats adjusted within twenty-four hours. It was interesting that as time went on the girls seemed to like this small house better than the big one. Both Joe and I noticed it. The only way I can explain it is that they seemed more tribal—following us from room to room, hanging out with us more.

It had been the right move for all of us.

I won't lie—I missed the Moscow house in many ways. But I loved the new house. It was so easy to live in—all on one level, even the laundry room. We had our first garage, and what a relief in Michigan winter to have that. I turned a walk-through area to the deck slider into my office, so all day I could look outside and see the most wonderful things.

The natural world at the ranch house was surprisingly different from what I saw out on the plain. At first I felt a little hemmed in with the tree lines all around the yard and so close to the house. The first month we lived there, I sat outside on the deck and heard an apple drop to the ground. It was so quiet in the yard that an apple thumping onto grass made me jump. A few days later I heard deer running through the swamp water behind the trees. I could not see them, only hear them. I found this enchanting.

Wildlife was constantly on the move through our property. Herds of deer strolled through and met at the pond. Sometimes a red fox would trot by the house. Turtles lived in the pond. We had not seen any of this in the Moscow yard—only the coyote outside my kitchen window. We had coyotes here too—we could hear them yipping at night, and one crossed the road when I was driving one day.

Wild turkey toms showed off and displayed for hens in our front yard. Occasionally a pair of mallards would try out the pond, and every now and then a red-tailed hawk would sail overhead or swoop down—I sometimes saw the shadow of his wingspan when I looked outside. We could hear sandhill cranes trilling as they flew overhead or gathered in the fields beyond the swamp. And on occasion we'd see a great blue heron hunting in the pond weeds.

The cats loved all this. We moved the huge kitty condo next to the slider, and it provided good viewing of the back yard. The girls tracked deer from window to window. They scratched on the slider glass when chipmunks and squirrels hung out on the deck. They enjoyed the many songbirds.

A friend of ours began calling our house the Surf Shack. Joe had always been a fan of California surf music, though he never surfed himself. But our friend gave him the moniker of Surfer Joe, and now Surfer Joe and I lived in the Surf Shack. It was no California, of course. Our surf was a pond full of the things that live in Michigan ponds and not big enough or clean enough to swim in. But it was our body of water here at the Surf Shack, and we liked it.

The hard year was coming to a close. Mom was gone. My sister Peg and I had the emotionally charged job of dealing with her estate—and Peg handled far more than I did. After she and I cleaned out the house in Florida, it got hit with two subsequent hurricanes—and there hadn't been a hurricane in that part of the state in a hundred years. Peg dealt with the damage. We planned to have a huge sale of Mom's possessions in Michigan, plus a lot of Joe's and mine, since we were conveniently downsizing at about the same time. Peg handled all this mostly herself since I was working. She cleaned out the Michigan house, set up all the items for the sale, and handled the publicity.

Then two days before the sale, Peg was hit by a truck while walking through a parking lot. It broke her knee. While she was recovering, Joe and I stepped in and switched the plan to an auction. It worked out, and we got the estate issues handled.

By Thanksgiving that year, I felt a deep, deep exhaustion. The weekend we were to pull out Christmas things, I told Joe it would have to wait. I couldn't do it yet. A few mornings later, while holding Lucy in my corner chair, I realized that there was nothing in me that could disrupt my home any more for any reason, not even for Christmas. Not right now. I needed to be still.

I asked Joe how he would feel if we didn't get a tree. He looked at me in surprise. "You want to decorate without it?"

I shook my head. "I don't want to do anything I don't have to do right now. There's nothing in me that can do anything extra."

Joe nodded. "If you aren't up to it, that's fine with me, because frankly, I'm overwhelmed too."

So we celebrated the holidays without fanfare. Friends and relatives gave us suggestions for downscaling the holiday rather than cutting out everything. My sister even brought over a small artificial tree to help us keep it simple. But I never unpacked it. It was important for me to see uncluttered surfaces, straight lines, calm colors. I couldn't even make myself haul out the stored boxes of Christmas wrapping paper and bows and bags. I simply went out and bought what I needed as I needed it.

After the holidays were over, things became emotionally tougher for me. The vision of my stronger, older sister down for the count and on painkillers after her accident so soon after watching Mom die had unnerved me. Peg got better, but for some reason, I couldn't get past it. And on top of that, I missed my mother terribly. During this time, when I needed to cry, I grabbed Kit Kat, held her close, and cried into her fur. Her purring was calming. Our little bundle of strong will had turned into a cuddle-bug and was always available for holding.

One morning I couldn't get out of bed. For three days I retreated to my bed as the cats stuck close by. When I came back to the world and forced myself back to work, that's all I did.

But something new had reared its head. When I left home in my car, I was back in that childhood thing of fearing the house would burn down while I was gone, now with the cats inside. Or someone would break in and do horrible things to the cats. The vivid ideations in my mind were frightening. It got so that I could not work through a list of errands away from home. Ever hopeful, I would make my list, but I could only handle one task at a time. Then I simply came home. Or if I had a little more left in me, I'd allow myself to do a drive-by to make sure everything looked okay, then drive back to town to handle the next thing on my list.

Then I came home from a three-day convention and couldn't remember what I did at the convention. It was as if the past few days were wiped clean from my memory. This happened following another conference a few weeks later. I had to look at my notes to trigger my memory about where I'd been and what I'd done.

Obviously concerned, I saw my medical doctor, who said, "Sometimes depression can affect short-term memory."

That was news to me. I thought I knew all the symptoms of depression. When she asked if I wanted to see the therapist in their clinic, I said I would, and what a good decision that was.

I entered talk therapy with Dr. Hawke, who for me became a compassionate voice of reason and one of my biggest cheerleaders. Plus he was an avid reader who enjoyed poetry. He even came to one of my poetry readings.

Thanks to my treatment with Dr. Hawke, my depression rolled away like the Red Sea. But something was left behind— the glaring anxiety I had never dealt with before. So now was the time to understand it with the help of Dr. Hawke. My anxiety improved with talk and the acceptance of my life as a good one.

The year anniversary of my mother's death came on a Monday. I dreaded its arrival, but it turned out that I would be hosting a work meeting in my house all that day. I was grateful people would be around. I woke up that morning to a steady, gentle rain that would last all day.

My guests arrived at the Surf Shack. While I made coffee, they fussed over Kit Kat and Lucy and remarked on the many windows. Then we sat at the table in the middle of the house for our meeting.

Something so sweet happened that day that I asked the

others to verify what I saw. In the back yard, then the front yard, then the back yard again, back and forth, a flock of cardinals, both male and female, played in the light rain. Only cardinals. We commented on it all day. On the first anniversary of my mother's death, once again I found a comfort I wasn't expecting.

·18·

GAME ON

The cat always leaves his mark upon his friends.

Spanish proverb

The Surf Shack was working out for us. It was closer to stores, activities, and even friends. It was safer to take walks near our house because we could avoid trucks. The move knocked a half hour off of Joe's commute, so now he drove forty-five minutes to work, all of it highway until the Ann Arbor exits.

We began to really like where we were. We no longer had the talks about where we would move if we could. We decided we were fine where we'd landed. We began attending a historic downtown Jackson church, and there we found a sense of community in a way we hadn't experienced since San Francisco.

We continued to note that the cats were quite happy with the new house. I would have thought that a smaller space would not be a good thing, but they still did everything they did in the old house. They window-hunted. They chased each other in the circle of rooms, through tunnels under the bed, and up and down the cat condo. I bought wicker armchairs for the dining table, and now the cats liked to do balancing acts on the backs and arms of the chairs. Not just Lucy—the more feet-on-ground Kit Kat walked on them too. She tended to follow Lucy's lead when it came to climbing and game-playing.

And Lucy was still teaching us new tricks and games at the Surf Shack. For one thing, she had become closer to Joe in the last couple of years. She used to watch Kit Kat interact with him, but I was her main human. Then two weeks after Mom died, I attended a conference in southern Indiana. I was gone seven days. When I returned, Lucy was at Joe's side. When I spoke to her, she looked at Joe. I tried again, and she would not look at me, only Joe. I was still a little fragile from losing Mom, and I went to the bedroom and actually cried when this happened. I heard Joe in the kitchen say, "Lucy, you're hurting your mother's feelings." That made me shift to laughing.

But it was true that during the week alone with Joe, Lucy decided he belonged to her as much as I did. After we moved, it was even more noticeable. She liked hanging out in his office. She began watching television with him, always approaching the couch from the top, walking the full length, then tucking herself in next to Joe on his left side, purring. She tucked in bottom first so it looked like she too was watching television, but she was simply expecting Joe to pet her. For hours, if Joe watched a movie.

When Lucy got overstimulated, she hopped down, groomed a bit, then did it all over again—approached from the top of the couch, dropped to Joe's left side, and so on. She completely ignored me at times like this, and I believe I was expected to leave the two of them alone, although Kit Kat was allowed to join them if she stayed on Joe's right side.

Lucy also somehow showed us in the Surf Shack that she liked riding on Joe's shoulders. How had we missed that all those years? Lucy now balanced herself on Joe's shoulder and hung onto his sweatshirt with her claws as he walked with her from room to room. She was always a high-places cat, so riding around on 6'2" Joe was quite awesome for her.

But our favorite new game she came up with was this one. Joe preferred to clean his razor while sitting on the bathroom floor. The bathroom sink and counter in the new house were quite low for some reason, especially for tall Joe. So when he cleaned his razor, he sat cross-legged on the floor and worked over the wastebasket, using the toilet lid as a surface to work from.

We observed that when Lucy heard two consecutive sounds—closing the lid to the commode followed by the sound of the plastic lid being removed from the razor—she knew it was time for razor-cleaning, and for some reason, Lucy was going to be there for it. If she heard the toilet lid go down, no matter where she was in the house, her head came up and one ear turned, waiting for the next sound, hoping for that rattling noise of a plastic razor cover. If it was not that, she'd go back to sleep. Or if she heard plastic without the first sound of the lid being lowered, no go. It must be in that specific order—toilet lid dropping followed by plastic rattling.

When she heard the lid go down, then heard the plastic, in that order, she stopped what she was doing and galloped to the bathroom. Once there, she rubbed against Joe while he petted her vigorously. Then she sprawled on her side, squawking and purring and bracing her legs to push against Joe while he continued to pet her. Obviously it took forever to clean a razor this way, but we concluded Lucy thought Joe was sitting on the floor and doing these actions *for* Lucy.

Of course we knew that cats must play in a way that feeds their need for prey activity. Lucy had always been more of a player in that way than Kit Kat, who tended to be a very sober cat and was by now more of a retiree in the hunting department. A typical feline, Lucy came to life at dawn and dusk, and during the morning hours she especially wanted to play. I needed to start work, so I finally learned to engage her while waiting for my pokey computer to boot up.

I learned from a cat expert how to handle a cat who seems to have an insatiable need for play. Play hard—really hard—for five minutes. Time it. Put aside the toy for two minutes. Play hard again for ninety seconds. Put away the toy for a minute. Play hard for thirty seconds. The end. It worked, and by then my computer was ready to roll too.

Sometimes when I used a fish line–style toy with Lucy, Kit Kat would watch from a hiding spot. Lucy could leap very high when excited, and it was fun to watch for both beast and human. But now and then, Kit Kat became so inspired by watching Lucy that she'd suddenly run in and take over. She seemed to remember the times of team hunting, and now she needed to make her move. So she gave one mighty pounce and "killed" the toy. Then she sat on it. Game over.

Unlike the rare reappearance of Kit Kat the Hunter, the

only time Lucy got that serious about real prey anymore was when she saw animals and songbirds outside. I learned how to tell what she was watching in the window without seeing it myself by her body language. If it was a bird, Lucy had a specific clicking and squawking noise in the back of her mouth. The first time I heard that back at the Moscow house, I thought I had the devil's cat.

If Lucy saw deer or humans outside, she watched their movements but not that enthusiastically. She didn't get too excited about wild turkeys either, unless they were close to the windows. With squirrels and chipmunks on the deck, Lucy literally threw herself at the slider. I actually saw her sit up once with her paws on the glass, and on the other side, a chipmunk sat up opposite Lucy with its paws on the glass.

But when Lucy saw a cat outdoors, even from a distance, she had a visceral and territorial response. The fur around her face, head, and neck puffed out like a sled dog's, and her tail grew huge. She'd slap that tail on a surface—it sounded like it had the weight of a plastic baseball bat—and she'd hiss and vocalize at the window. My peacemaker cat turned into something else.

When we moved to the Surf Shack, Lucy kicked up her game and developed misplaced aggression. Once I started to move her from the window in the middle of the night when she was growling and yowling over a cat outside, and Lucy turned and bit me. Usually, though, she went after the only cat available to her—poor Kit Kat. It could get ugly, and then we had to separate them. It got so when Kit Kat observed Lucy getting cranked up over what was clearly a cat outside, Kit Kat would huddle under the dining table with the most hapless look on her face, just waiting for what was going to happen unless we stopped it in time. No longer at those times was she the dominant cat.

One summer night while I was traveling and Joe was home, Lucy must have seen something cat-like, because she threw herself at the slider screen, screaming. The screen popped out. Suddenly Lucy was outside in the dark for the first time at the Surf Shack. When Joe realized what had happened, he quickly shut Kit Kat in a room and grabbed a flashlight.

Once outdoors, Joe could not see Lucy—we had no outside lighting. But he knew that if he called her name, she'd answer. She'd started doing that with him since moving to the Surf Shack. Joe called her, and he heard her signature squawk from around the corner of the house. He spied her in the dark and approached carefully, knowing that if he messed up, Lucy might shoot into the woods. He told me he thought of *Apollo 13* and the line "Failure is not an option."

Joe managed to pounce fast enough to grab Lucy and hold her firm. Her adrenaline was so high, she screamed all the way to the house. Once inside, Joe closed the slider, released Kit Kat from her room, and went to the couch, where he turned on the TV as if nothing had happened. Once again he understood his cats in his calm way. Within a few minutes, here came both cats, showing up at opposite ends of the couch, as usual. They each positioned themselves next to Joe in their preferred spots—Lucy on the left, Kit Kat on the right. All was well.

I am so glad I missed that.

The girls got out of the house one more time, and that needed to be the last time for me. The slider screen was accidentally left open one summer night, and by the time we noticed, both cats were outside in the dark. I was panicked. We ran out to the deck and almost tripped over them. Both Kit Kat and Lucy were crouching down and looking up at the star-filled sky. It had been a long time since the stars were over their heads, and they seemed mesmerized.

Joe grabbed Lucy, I grabbed the slower Kit Kat, and all was okay. But we made two changes after that. We installed a deck light and a back yard light, and we figured out a way to help ourselves see at a glance if the slider screen was open or closed. We had some leftover wood slats in a criss-cross pattern that previous owners had used to skirt the deck. Joe nailed a portion of that to the bottom of the slider screen, and it looked fine and provided a bit of a barrier. The girls could still see out and enjoy the fresh air between criss-cross slats.

I felt bad about this, as if I'd just denied them some of their window viewing. But once again, I wasn't thinking like a cat. They actually preferred watching the yard from behind the wood slats. Why? They could watch the yard and breathe in fresh air all while hidden. They were cats, after all.

By the next year's Christmas, I was doing better. Dr. Hawke had been a great help. Work was going well. I was making new friends and keeping in better touch with the old. Joe and I were involved in activities at church. Joe had become the sound man, and I began singing in the choir.

A long time ago, I was a professional singer on the side. But I hadn't really sung much in twenty-five years. Even for choral singing, I needed to get my vocal instrument back in shape, especially since we had a cantata coming up this year. So while waiting for Joe to come home one night, I washed dishes and sang. I had Handel's *Messiah* on and was following along—until I heard a plaintive cry. It was the particular meow I recognized as Lucy's heads-up that there may be vomiting.

The considerate thing about Lucy was that if she did up-chuck, I could count on her leaping to the floor and giving me enough lead time to catch it in process in a napkin. Then she always walked a few steps and did it again, and I could catch it again. Was this one of those times?

I turned from the dishes and wiped my hands on a towel. Lucy sat on the buffet, watching me. "Are you okay, sweetie?"

Lucy stayed put and simply averted her face.

Then I got it—my cat wasn't sick to her stomach. She just didn't like my singing. She wanted me to stop. As we know, Lucy the Peacemaker hated loud noise and apparently classified me as a producer of such. So if she couldn't save others, she could at least save herself and her sensitive ears.

I heard myself say to my cat, "I am *not* that bad."

Lucy glanced at me, hopped down, and trotted away. Her work was done.

Everyone's a critic.

Lucy's disapproval aside, I was also enthusiastic about these upcoming holidays because this year I had worked very hard so that I could take time off work starting one week before Christmas and not return until after the new year.

The time off arrived. That first day, I was so excited I was like a little kid who doesn't know which fun thing to do first. That lasted two days. Then I got hit hard with a sinus infection—something I had never had before in my life. It left me literally sleepless for two weeks.

Just as my round of antibiotics was finishing, I got a separate virus that kept me up coughing at night for four more weeks. For six weeks—through Christmas, New Year's, my January birthday, and then some—I was sick to some degree every single day. I constantly reminded myself that it was all temporary, just weird and unfortunate timing. But I felt like a little kid once again—this time, one who doesn't get to go to the party. Joe slept on the futon in the living room for weeks because of my coughing.

For all of her life indoors, Kit Kat slept with us. At some point in the night, she'd hop onto the end of the bed and walk up the middle between us to the head of the bed. Then she curled on her side like a little person, her head resting on her own small pillow tucked between Joe's and my pillows. She liked to stay warm and connected. Joe and I were purred to sleep many a night and purred awake in the morning.

Even though Kit Kat slept with the two of us, she still favored Joe. So on the first night Joe slept in the living room because of my coughing, I shut the bedroom door, expecting Kit Kat would join Joe. Then I saw her black velvety paw reach under the door. I opened the door. Kit Kat sat back at the threshold and looked up at me. Then she looked over her shoulder toward the living room. She looked back up at me.

"Sorry, sweetie," I told her. "We're not together tonight. Did you want to come in?"

She did. As I lay back down, Kit Kat hopped onto the bed as usual and walked up the middle to her pillow. But this time she did something different. She sat at her pillow and watched me. I lay down on my left side facing Kit Kat and immediately began coughing. She observed this for a bit, then she turned herself completely around so that she was facing me and the other end of the bed. She hooked both her front paws over my arm and settled her body down like a camel. She kept her paws hooked over my arm while I coughed. Literally, she hung on to my arm.

When I finished coughing, Kit Kat leaned her face against my upper arm and went to sleep. She ignored her pillow. She did not sleep in the way she had slept for all her years. Instead, she turned herself completely around and seemed to attend to me. That is how we slept most of that night.

The next night I assumed she'd be with Joe. Not so. I settled in on my left side, and here came my bundle of concern walking up the center of the bed. Again, she walked to the head of the bed, then turned completely around to face me. She hooked her paws over my lower arm and watched me for a while, then leaned against me to sleep.

I called Joe in. I wanted a witness to this change in behavior in our OCD cat. He confirmed it, and this went on for the next six weeks. Every night that Joe bunked on the futon, I got into bed and lay on my left side, and here came Kit Kat up the middle of the bed. But she never slept curled on her side with her head on her pillow during those weeks; rather, she slept hunkered down on my arm. When I turned over to my right side, she then turned on her left side, her warm, purring body pressed against my back like a hot water bottle.

If I had a particularly tough coughing spell, Kit Kat would wake up and hang on while I hacked away. Sometimes I woke up in the night because I couldn't breathe freely. So I sat up for a while against the pillows. Kit Kat sat up too, right next to me. We watched TV together, sometimes most of the night, until I could go back to sleep. Clearly we had a working cat that winter. She was Kit Kat the Comforter, my personal nurse. Joe said he envisioned her in a little old-fashioned blue cape and nurse's cap with a red cross on it.

I eventually got better, and one night, Kit Kat did not come to the bed. She slept with Joe in the living room instead of with me. That night the cough was controllable, and I slept good and hard for the first time in weeks. I suspected the bad stuff was over and that somehow Kit Kat knew it. She continued to sleep with Joe for the next couple nights, and I continued to get better. Soon we all slept in the same bed together again, and then Kit Kat curled on her side, her head back on her little pillow between Joe and me.

After that winter, Kit Kat never again slept with me in the way she slept with me when I was ill—facing me, hanging on to my arm with her front legs. But I suspected if I needed her comforting abilities in the future, she'd put her little nursing cape and cap on again and be right there. On duty.

·19·

OLDER, SWEETER, CRANKIER

Always the cat remains a little beyond
the limits we try to set for him in our
blind folly.

Andre Norton

Kit Kat was living a good long life as an FIV kitty. But like
many cats, she began visibly aging after about eight or nine
years. Our first hint was that she became a sweet little old
lady. She had had such a strong and dominant personality all
of her life that it was interesting to watch her mellow with
age. She was always available for holding and cuddling. She
appreciated things we did to make her life easier and had a
certain *thank-you* look she would give us.

As Kit Kat aged, she began sleeping in the sun as much as
possible, often in the living room where sun poured through

a huge picture window. When I was home, I would pick her up and move her so she could stay in the sunlight. Even startled awake from a sound sleep, she understood what I was doing and was appreciative. Once I'd moved her into the warmth, she flashed me her *thank-you* look and went back to sleeping—something she was doing more and more.

One day Kit Kat didn't join us at night on the bed; instead she slept in a cat bed under the bed. I thought maybe she was feeling cold at night now. We kept cat beds down there for hiding and for keeping warm next to a register. But after several days of Kit Kat not doing what she'd done almost every day of her indoor life, I noticed—finally—that it wasn't just the bed. She wasn't jumping up on anything. She was suffering from joint pain, and it hurt too much for her to get on the bed. The only way she could get me to understand was not to sleep with us.

That day I bought her a set of pet stairs—four carpeted steps. When I brought it home, Kit Kat watched me park the item at the foot of the bed. She immediately marched up the four steps to the top of the bed, sat down, and flashed me her *thank-you* look. No hesitation, no sniffing the steps over. She knew this was hers.

After that, I placed small stools all over the house next to anything she might want to jump on. We also added the joint-friendly glucosamine supplement Cosequin to her food and saw the vet more frequently—he performed pet acupuncture when necessary and kept an eye on our girl.

I had noticed that Kit Kat wasn't afraid of noises like she used to be. When the lawn guys came to mow, she no longer headed under the bed until they were gone. I thought maybe this second house didn't hold certain fearful memories for her. Donna, Pet Expert, set me straight. "Kit Kat's not young anymore," she said, "and she's not hearing low tones." Of course, Donna was right. It got so Kit Kat would sit right on the bed and watch us while we vacuumed the bedroom.

Lucy was a year and a half younger than Kit Kat. She enjoyed good health and mobility right into her older years, and that was a relief. But Lucy's personality changed with age too. My sweet playful cat was becoming cranky. I would never have believed it possible. She even had Mean Girl moments where she sat on the top step of the pet stairs so Kit Kat couldn't get on the bed. If Kit Kat tried to move around Lucy, Lucy batted the top of Kit Kat's head really fast as if she were dribbling a basketball, glaring at her sister the whole time. Our once-mighty Kit Kat would, of all things, retreat.

I scolded Lucy about this, and my goodness what a haughty look I got in return. I remember saying to Joe, "What happened to my sweet little scamper cat? Who *is* this cat?"

This was a reminder that we lived with animals. Dominance was shifting.

As part of my job as an acquisitions editor in a publishing house, I attended writers conferences, looking for books to acquire for possible publication. A literary agent sent me a link one day to something called the Cat Writers Association. We were experimenting with publishing animal-themed books at the time at the publishing house, and the agent thought I might be interested that the CWA had a conference coming up. I had not heard of this organization. It had been going on for twenty years, and somehow I missed it. I signed up to attend as a book editor.

The CWA conference was held in Los Angeles that year in an airport hotel. I showed up, not knowing anyone, and at first, it occurred to me I might have been dropped into some Egyptian cat cult. Let's just say they liked their cats. As a newbie, I was called a "kitten." There was a lot of animal print clothing milling around me, which I noticed with a secret smirk. Imagine my surprise when I glanced in a mirror and realized that in fact I too was wearing animal print.

Within half an hour, however, it was clear that I was among publishing pros. Never was there a more focused convention than this in my personal experience. The magazine *Cat Fancy* was there as well as lots of other animal publications plus shelter organizations and breeders. There were far more cat publications and cat-themed websites than I was aware of. I remember that it was at that conference that the *Cat Fancy* people declared *litterbox* to be one word. Make a note. We did in our editorial department back home.

The goal of CWA was to raise the status of the cat through professional writing and art, and they did exactly that. They endorsed good living for the cat as they worked to increase understanding of the feline. I saw a lot of talent, creativity, and substance.

And the CWA members were fun. The membership was predominantly female, though I met men there too. These women didn't mind being seen as Crazy Cat Ladies—they had a great collective sense of humor about it. On banquet night, there was a speech from the president. At one table, when they liked what the speaker said, they meowed. When they didn't, they hissed.

I became a member of the Cat Writers Association.

A year or so later, I noticed that Kit Kat was traveling around the house oddly. She no longer crossed a room. To navigate now, she circled the room and kept a wall close to her left side. Had she had a stroke? I took her to the vet clinic.

Our Jackson clinic had three or four vets at any time, but we usually asked for one in particular when it came to Kit Kat. Dr. Tim seemed to have a special connection to her. He had had temperamental torties himself, and the first time he dealt with Kit Kat I remember he stroked her while she hissed and growled. She was already letting him know she didn't like this one bit. Dr. Tim smiled and said, "I love you too, Kit Kat."

Of course we knew how our girl was so touchy about claw trims. Dr. Tim experimented with a number of ways to do those. Once Kit Kat bit him and drew blood. I was horrified, but he said, "That was my fault." Eventually, maybe because of my nervous energy, he would take her in the back of the clinic and trim her. I always trusted him to handle Kit Kat without me in the room.

One time Dr. Tim was gone with Kit Kat for about ten minutes, and I wondered what was wrong. He apologized when he brought her back. "I grabbed a ringing phone, and it turned out I needed to talk to the person. So Kit Kat sat on my lap while I talked."

Well, there was little our Kit Kat enjoyed more than sitting on one's lap while they were on the phone. When I traveled and called home at night, Joe often had Kit Kat on his lap. He'd put the phone up to her ear while I said her name over and over. She rubbed her cheek on the receiver and purred. On my end, it sounded like Christmas paper being wadded up.

Now Dr. Tim showed me that Kit Kat had cataracts. She wasn't completely blind, but she was close to it, enough that she felt more secure hugging the wall on her left side when walking.

Back home I watched her maneuver the living room by circling around it, leaning to the left, and I started to cry. Then I stopped. I knew blind people. In fact, I grew up with a blind cousin who used to climb trees with us. And at my second CWA convention, I met a blind cat named Spirit.[*] Even completely blind, Spirit was all cat. He was leash-trained, and I watched him walk through a crowded hotel lobby ahead of his human, ears moving, nose and whiskers twitching. He sat next to me on a couch, and when I reached over to touch his big, gorgeous paw, he batted me. Even blind, he liked prey play.

So I stopped my tears. My resilient cat had already figured out how to handle her near-blindness, and she was getting around fine. I needed to pull back my anxious energy, move a few things in the house to help her navigate, and keep an eye out for her.

A month later, Kit Kat began losing weight and acting lethargic. Dr. Tim ran tests and found that she was in renal failure. This is not unusual for older cats, and we worked to extend her life and keep her feeling good. But soon I feared she wouldn't make it through the month, because our little hunger marcher would not eat the special kidney diet food. Such foods are low in protein of necessity, and we tried them all. She'd eat a little bit of special kibble out of my hand, but I always had the sense she was eating it to be polite.

*You can read about Spirit's fascinating story and further adventures online at https://www.facebook.com/spirit.ablindcat.

This was a problem. She wasn't going to survive if she didn't eat. Another vet at the clinic remembered that during the pet food scare, they couldn't get special kidney diet food, and she suggested we try a popular brand of cat food for mature cats over seven years of age. The ingredients were similar to kidney diet food. So I brought home some tuna gravy in that brand, and Kit Kat cleaned it right up. Then she looked up at me. I fed her more, and she cleaned that up. Our girl was hungry. Our eager eater was back.

The other thing that helped Kit Kat's quality of life was subcutaneous fluids, which she at first received every other week at the vet's. Between eating again and fluids, Kit Kat actually gained weight over the winter. She was almost blind, almost deaf (we spoke to her in a loud, high register now), arthritic, and in renal failure. But she was still our happy girl.

Donna gave us a list of things to consider in terms of end-of-life quality—is your pet eating, drinking, eliminating appropriately, recognizing you, enjoying being around you . . . ? Yes to all. And still "watching" TV with us, still sleeping with us, still insisting on being fed on schedule. In other words, still Kit Kat.

One winter day, she wasn't in any of her warm spots—in the sun or in her bed by the register. Then I saw her snuggled up to the front door's threshold. It was drafty there, and I couldn't understand why she was doing that. I took a picture and emailed it to Donna. She called and said, "Don't you ever kick the covers off? She got too warm and found a way to cool off." I felt like saying, "Duh."

We had a good winter with Kit Kat, then age fifteen. She was sleeping very close to me at night. She shifted from using her pillow to putting her head in the crook of my arm for sleeping. I loved that. I realized that she had slept next to my face for almost a fourth of my life. Spring came, and Kit Kat remained with us, a determined little girl who seemed to understand that we were trying to help her feel better. And she grew even sweeter.

One spring night I baked salmon for dinner. In the past, I would give a bite to Kit Kat, but I didn't anymore because of the kidney issues. After dinner, I soaked the plates in some dishwater and left the Pyrex baking dish with some remaining bites of salmon on the stovetop to deal with later. Then I went into the bedroom to watch a show on TV.

Half an hour later, Joe walked in and said, "Why is Kit Kat on the counter?"

Kit Kat didn't get on counters. In fact, how could she get up there with all her issues? Yet there she was, sitting in front of the coffeemaker, grooming her face. We slowly realized that she smelled the salmon—her olfactory sense was working just fine—and she wanted some.

It was a pretty big climb for a lame and almost blind cat. We figured she started at my reading chair where there was a little stool for her. Onto the ottoman, up the arm of the reading chair, onto the windowsill, lean to the left against the glass as she passed the window, step up on the counter, lean to the left again, which took her through the dishwater (her feet and tail were wet), past the coffeemaker, onto the stove. Eureka!—leftover chunks of salmon. She was still washing the remnants off her cheeks when we saw her.

"How on earth could she do that?" I said.

"Extreme food boredom," Joe responded.

We agreed that our cat wanted to live. So we would continue to help her live as long as it made sense.

Ernest Hemingway said, "Every true story ends in death." It's his conclusion that any storyteller who bypasses the reality of death in a story cannot be trusted. And maybe he's right. So I will tell you what you already suspect, that we eventually had to have Kit Kat put to sleep.

I had never put an animal down. Neither had Joe. People talked about it. People sometimes couldn't get over it. I had a lot of fear of that day.

But for Kit Kat's sake, Joe and I also didn't want to wait too long. We knew well-meaning people could hold on when they should let go, and then their pet suffered but was hardwired not to show it. I prayed specifically that it would be obvious when the time came to let go of Kit Kat. I still traveled for work, often gone several days at a time. Before each trip, I would hold Kit Kat close and whisper in her ear: "Don't you die while I'm gone." And she didn't.

It would turn out that the day Kit Kat had to leave us would not be the worst day of our lives—because fortunately, it wound up being one of Kit Kat's best days.

Kit Kat had gotten to where she was getting fluids twice a week. The day came, however, when Dr. Tim said, "I'm concerned. She's dehydrated. Let's see in a few days if she retains today's fluids." I thought she seemed especially tired. Still moving forward, still determined, but tired. Joe agreed. We thought she had in fact taken a turn, but again, we weren't sure.

Two days later at noon, I fed Kit Kat in the kitchen. We had a way of doing this now where she'd receive a little wet food, eat it up, and then look at me for more. It seemed easier on her digestion to feed her slowly. I was about to give her the second helping when suddenly she backed up and looked around with terror in her eyes. I had seen Kit Kat hallucinate twice before from a certain medication, so I recognized that she was hallucinating now.

And then right away she had a severe seizure. It literally threw her around the kitchen, and I had to move out of the way as she flopped up and down for probably ten long seconds. The thumping on the floor was so loud that Lucy came in from the bedroom to see what was going on.

It broke my heart to watch this happen to my frail cat. When it ended, I thought it had killed her. But it hadn't, so I covered her and called in an emergency message to the vet clinic.

Lucy sniffed Kit Kat's blanket, then crouched down a couple feet away and kept her eye on her sister. I could see Kit Kat's breathing was steady now under the blanket, so I picked her up and put her in her carrier—I figured she would be safer there if it happened again—and considered the situation.

One thing was crystal clear, as I had prayed it would be. This was the day we would have to say good-bye to our girl. We could not protect Kit Kat from having seizures like that. What if I were traveling? What if she were on a higher surface when she had a seizure and fell and hurt herself? I had a million "what if" scenarios, and it all added up to one thing: There could be no more seizures. This was the day we'd have to let her go. I called Joe and asked him to come home and told him why. He was home in an hour.

By then, Kit Kat seemed to be wondering why she was in her carrier. I realized that, like many people who have seizures, she probably didn't remember it. So Joe took her out of her carrier and held her while I talked to the clinic.

They confirmed that seizures like this would most certainly happen again, and there was nothing to be done about it.

Years ago, we had made a plan for this day. We had asked Dr. Tim if he would come to the house when the time came, and he promised he would. Now he called and said he'd be there after a farm appointment, at about six.

Joe and I spent the next four hours loving on our Kit Kat, and she loved on us right back. It was a warm day in May, and we opened all the windows. Kit Kat lay on my chest next to an open window and dozed. After a while, Joe took her to the bedroom to nap with him. He placed her under the covers, spooned against him, something she always loved.

At some point, she woke up and indicated that she was hungry. So I fed her all the fishy cat food she loved but lately couldn't have—what difference would it make now? She licked her lips and gave me her look that said, "More, please." I gave her more. She sat and groomed for a bit, then curled up on me and dozed.

Joe and I traded her off a couple more times. Kit Kat seemed thrilled to be cuddling with us both so much. I held her and squeezed her and talked to her. I told her how much I loved her. I thanked her for being my baby. I thanked her for walking back to us those many years ago and taking such good care of Joe and me. At one point, Kit Kat woke up from dozing on my chest. She stretched straight up on her front legs, then turned to the window and breathed in the fresh air. She looked back at me for a long time, eye to eye. It was a different look on her face—it seemed both loving and knowing. I felt she was saying good-bye. Then she turned away from the window, curled up on me again, and slept.

When Dr. Tim came, Kit Kat was in the bed with Joe.

That's where we said good-bye to her, in Joe's spot. When it was over, we brought Lucy to Kit Kat, but she didn't want to sniff her. She hurried under the bed, away from us. Lucy had uncharacteristically been staying under the bed for days, and that's where she wanted to be now. Later I realized that Lucy had known Kit Kat was dying long before this day. Lucy would stay under the bed for several more days.

When Dr. Tim picked up Kit Kat's body to take her with him, he stopped and smiled gently. "You know, this is the first time Kit Kat hasn't gotten mad at me when I picked her up."

Joe and I watched from the window as Dr. Tim's truck drove away with our girl. Then we wrapped our arms around each other and bawled like babies.

·20·

THE TEXANS

Every life should have nine cats.

Anonymous

Lucy eventually came out from under the bed. She seemed to grieve for a few days, and then she stopped. In fact, we were surprised to see that she seemed to like having us to herself. We didn't think it would last, so we watched and waited. We believed she'd want a new feline friend, but it would be up to her.

When I was in high school, a stray tomcat came through the broken basement window and moved in with us. He charmed us completely, though we had to get him neutered so he'd stop spraying the drapes. My mother was quite patient about that, I must say.

We named him Tom. Yes, we were an original lot with

the pet names. Tom had that friendly, assertive way of a big orange male, and he and my stepdad were absolute buddies. He followed Dad around, indoors or outdoors, like a friendly little dog, one might say.

Tom and my beloved cat Boots got along well enough. No love lost, but no fighting either. When Boots was killed by a car, it took only a week or so before Tom brought us a replacement cat. He led an injured female into the house via the basement window. She was a very nice tuxedo cat with a torn ear and some other minor injuries. Tom fussed over her until we got her fixed up, and she was allowed to stay. Then he pretty much ignored her.

I always remembered that. For whatever his reasons, Tom wanted another one of his species around. I figured Lucy would want a companion, and Joe and I would follow her lead as to when.

Two months after Kit Kat died, we were away for a full week. Our cat-sitter stayed at the house the whole time—we especially wanted Lucy to have as much attention as possible right then. Nevertheless, when we returned, we found the usually aloof Lucy was uncharacteristically clingy. The time had come to find another cat.

I drove to a shelter in Jackson and completed an application. I wanted a young adult male, and that day, two of them at the shelter vied for my attention. But for some reason, the minute either of them got in a closed room with me, they wanted nothing—and I mean nothing—to do with me. One ignored my hand while I tried to pet him and paid no attention even when I threw him a toy. He just sniffed all the corners of the room and the floor the entire visit. The other one kept jumping up to the window, bouncing over and over, in hopes of getting out of there. So much for my cat cred. This was not the day for a cat to come home with me.

Then strangely, Joe and I each came up with the same idea but separately. We each thought we should adopt littermate kittens. That way we could raise up a new generation, and maybe they'd be spirited companions for Lucy.

I asked for the opinion of Spirit the Blind Cat's "Mom" in Texas, and she thought it was a good idea. I went on the lookout for littermates, but in spite of the push these days to buy local, I wound up getting kittens from Texas.

It so happened that that spring Spirit's Mom had taken in not one but two abandoned pregnant cats, and they each had given birth to five kittens. Then she learned that there was an abandoned litter of kittens at a construction site, but nobody was certain where the litter was located at that site.

Enter Spirit the Blind Cat to the rescue. He and Mom and a friend went to the construction site, and Mom took Spirit off his leash under the temporary construction building on the site. He listened and sniffed around and almost immediately signaled that he heard or smelled something in the floor above. Mom and her friend had belly-crawled in under the building, so now they pulled at the subfloor insulation according to Spirit's lead. A kitten's head popped up. There were four kittens about ten days old. They'd been huddled together in the cold with no sustenance for over thirty-two hours after their feral mother had been captured and taken away. It was a miracle they were still alive.

The four kittens went to Spirit's house. Would the two foster momma cats nurse them? Yes, but it was a labor of love and partnership by Spirit's Mom and the surrogate mommas. Eventually both cats nursed the new babies, and everyone thrived.

When I talked to Spirit's Mom about our plan to get littermate kittens, she said, "Aren't you coming to Texas for a conference? Why don't you adopt two of mine? You know they're healthy and very well-adjusted."

I ran it by Joe, and he approved. So from photographs of the fourteen available kittens, I picked two of the construction site littermates. I flew to Texas for my conference, and when I returned, I brought onboard a pair of three-month-old kittens—one black, one silver tabby. They huddled together in their comfy carrier, tucked in next to my feet. They never made a peep the entire trip. My secure babies flew far better than I do.

That night when Joe picked us up curbside, two pairs of golden eyes peered up at him in the dark. He grinned back at them. "Well, aren't you two cute?" he said. We named the black kitten Tiki Spirit and the silver tabby Mary Katherine—calling her Mary Kat as a nod to Kit Kat. They were the most sociable creatures Joe and I had ever met. We fell in love with them immediately.

Not so much Lucy. We did all the right things—we kept the kittens separate from Lucy at first, then tried bringing them together. Lucy was not having any of it. She parked herself in the living room, the farthest room from theirs, and stayed on the couch for weeks.

Then one day Lucy moved to the center of the house so she could watch the kittens. They really wanted to interact with her, but our cranky old girl wanted this done her own way. Lucy hissed and did smackdowns on the babies when they tried to get close to her, dribbling on their little heads with her paw until they retreated. She truly only wanted to watch. Sometimes she watched with an inscrutable Cheshire cat expression, but her curiosity about them was quite clear.

And the Texans treated Lucy like royalty. They followed her around the house and stared at her in absolute fascination. They acted like she was the most beautiful thing they'd ever seen in their young lives. They would even watch her use the litterbox and then flank her exit path, gazing up at her as she walked between them as if she were a magnificent ocean liner leaving port. Having been socialized in Texas around adult cats, Tiki and Mary Kat knew how to maintain a respectful distance from the Queen.

While they were kittens, we kept the babies confined in their room at night. Then the morning came when Lucy parked herself at their threshold and meowed at me. She wanted them out. Now. Again, she wanted to watch them.

On a Saturday morning six weeks after the kittens arrived, I heard Lucy run the length of the house with a heavy footfall. It was the kind of running that said, "Pay attention to me!" She ran back through the house the same way, and the kittens understood. Lucy wanted them to give chase, and they did. I watched the three of them play and run all over the futon in the living room. Soon enough, they all slept on the bed together, like a little pride of lions among the linens. Although Lucy would sleep mere inches from Tiki and Mary Kat, they still were not to touch her, and they knew it.

The kittens were working out even better than I had hoped. They made Joe and me play with them, much like Lucy had when she was young. But the best thing the sweet Texans did was help Lucy find her youth again, both mentally and physically. I had been worried after Kit Kat died that Lucy would not be far behind, simply because she was aging. But Tiki and Mary Kat kept Lucy on her toes, and it was as if her aging stopped. They were her fountain of youth.

Shortly after Lucy turned fifteen, I could not find her one day. She did not come when I called. I searched for her until, in the living room, I finally heard her squawk. I looked up, and there sat Lucy atop a six-foot-high bookcase. She had never gone up there before, and now she was waiting for me to notice.

"What are you doing up there, Lucy?"

Squawk.

"Can you come down?"

Squawk.

She hopped down to a windowsill and from there hopped to the floor. Then she strolled out of the room, her point made: "I'm still amazing. Don't forget it."

Recently I sat on the bed and watched Lucy play a territorial game with her sisters. Every time either Tiki or Mary Kat tried to jump on the bed, Lucy smacked her down with her signature dribbling paw action. Over and over Lucy did this, running from one side of the bed to the other, eyes bright, tail twitching, having the best time.

She stopped suddenly and looked at me for a few seconds until her own twitching tail caught her eye. She turned and stared at it as if she'd never seen it before.

And then my fifteen-year-old Lucy chased her tail. Around and around, like she did when she was young, every now and then stopping to look me in the eye, then running in circles again. The Texans watched from the floor, their golden eyes wide, enthralled with their big whirling-dervish sister.

Maybe Lucy wanted to impress them. But I believe that when my beautiful, cranky, sweet blue cat chased her tail like she did when she was a youngster, she did it just for me.

ACKNOWLEDGMENTS

Many, many thanks to the talented people at Revell, a division of Baker Publishing Group, for their enthusiastic, good work. Huge thanks to my Revell acquisitions editor and fellow Cat Woman, Dr. Vicki Crumpton, who understands authors and animals and treats both with tremendous kindness and finesse. Big thanks to Jennifer Leep, Baker Publishing Group's Executive Vice President of Trade Books, for her encouragement and consistent support. More big thanks to project editor Laura Peterson, marketing manager Twila Bennett, and publicity manager Claudia Marsh for their very good care. Also thanks to Dave Lewis, Mark Rice, Nathan Henrion, Rob Teigen, Michele Misiak, Janelle Mahlmann, Karen Steele, Erin Bartels, Andrea Doering, Kelsey Bowen, and Max Eerdmans for their collective vision. Thanks to Jennifer Nutter, who always listens to me. Thanks to fellow Cat Woman Cheryl Van Andel for the "paw-some" cover and to Dan Malda and his team for their fine interior design. Thanks also to Minnesota Cat Man Steve Oates for his encouragement. And extra thanks to Michigan Cat Man Dwight Baker, President of Baker Publishing Group, for publishing me.

Loving thanks to my sister and brother-in-law, Peggy and Dick Lowe, for their ongoing support. Loving thanks also to favorite cousin Pat Schaible for always cheering me on. I gratefully acknowledge the love and pride expressed toward me by my beloved parents and stepparents who have all passed on—my father Otho K. Hull, my mother Mildred M. Smith, my stepfather Albert M. Smith, and my stepmother Virginia Hull. I miss them all.

Thanks to those animal experts who have generously given me advice and encouragement, including the dedicated staff of Jackson, Michigan's Blackman Animal Clinic, the talented members of the Cat Writers Association, the miracle-working Mom of Spirit the Blind Cat, and the irrepressible Donna Acton, LVT. Thanks to my out-of-town animal-loving friends Mary Rooney, Dan Noreen, Claudia Wolfe St. Clair, Donna Lowe, Mary Busha, Nancy Angelo, Donna Kehoe, Jeanette Thomason, Karen Gier, and Sara Fortenberry for their encouragement. Thanks to Nancy Demeter for the Surf Shack. Thanks to Dog Woman Ev Lazaroff, who listens to my cat stories and seems to enjoy them. Thanks to Michelle Sawyer, whose sweet ink sketches on napkins of Kit Kat and Lucy kept me going on the hard days. And a very grateful hug to "Aunt" Mary Ann Osborn, the best cat-sitter in the world, in spite of her allergy to cats.

Special thanks to Lenore Person at Guideposts for catching the vision for the book and kicking me into motion. Thanks to the people of The First Congregational Church of Jackson for being so supportive of my writing. Thanks to the members of Columbia Women Writers, Ann Arbor Hens with Pens, Chelsea Lifestories Group, Monday Dream Group, and various Michigan poetry groups that included M. L. Liebler, Ann Green, John Wood, Marijo Grogan, Martha Petry, and Kawita Kandpal, among others. And finally, I wish my dear friends Mary C. Barber, Ila J. Smith, and Maria Orlowski were alive so I could thank them for their absolute faith in my writing.

Lonnie Hull DuPont is an award-winning poet, book editor, and writer. Her poetry has been nominated for a Pushcart Prize, and she is the author of several books of nonfiction, including five compilations of animal stories under the pseudonym of Callie Smith Grant. A member of the Cat Writers Association, she lives in rural Michigan with her husband and their cats.

"In that moment, I realized that healing had begun.
That cat didn't need something from me.
I needed something from him."

Two charming collections of stories
that honor the companionship, humor, and sense
of mystery that a cat can bring to our lives.

"I had no doubt that whoever had been out there had meant to harm me, but had been foiled by one small, determined dog."

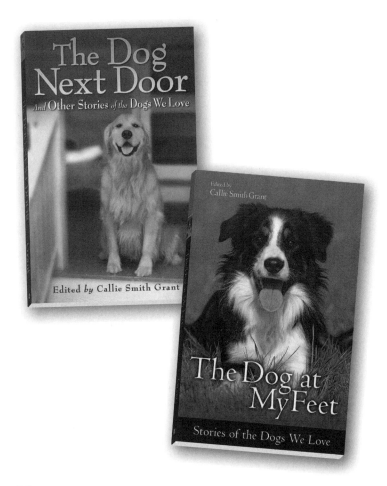

There is no more loyal buddy than a dog. These two heartwarming collections of stories celebrate the joy, laughter, and sweetness that dogs bring to our lives.

 Revell
a division of Baker Publishing Group
www.RevellBooks.com

Available wherever books and ebooks are sold.

Few creatures are as noble and soul-stirring as the horse. They give us a taste of wildness and yet make us feel at home.

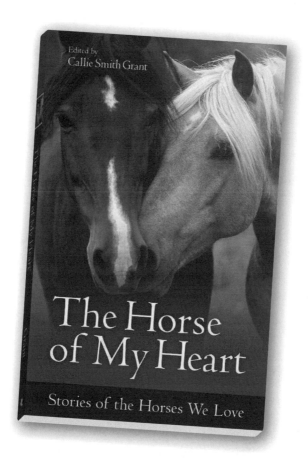

This beautiful collection of stories will inspire and move us in the same way these marvelous beasts capture our hearts and imagination.